FATHERS, ARISE!

A CLARION CALL TO GOD'S STEWARDS TO SALVAGE THE NEXT GENERATION.

By

KOLA OLADEJI

Table of Contents

Dedication

This book is dedicated to God, the Father of all fathers, Abba, the Source of all things.

He is the Father of our Lord Jesus Christ, and by the privilege of adoption, He is also my Heavenly Father. I am so glad I can boldly say, Abba, Father!

He is the epitome of a great father and the only one who could wear the badge of the Perfect Father.

He separated me from my mother's womb and called me through His grace to reveal His Son in me, that I might declare His counsel to my generation and the next.

To Him alone be all the glory forever for doing this work in and through me, Amen!

God, in His infinite wisdom, also positioned me under the tutelage of one of His finest, visionary leaders and Pastors; Pastor Toye & Wumi Ademola, the Presiding Pastors of Dominion International Center, Worldwide, with the headquarters based in Houston, Texas, and several other branches across the globe.

Acknowledgments

It is of utmost importance for me to acknowledge God's unusual kindness extended to me in the investment of Jesus Christ, the BEST of heaven offered to bring me in, and the Holy Spirit, the ALL of heaven, to keep me in; I am eternally grateful for my salvation.

In God's deep wisdom, He has made me a product of many fathers who have been very generous in playing their roles in shaping and sharpening me for the assignments I am called to do.

The first on the row of my fathers is the Late Mr. Babatunde Oladeji, my biological father, the man who did his best to give me the life he did not have. He imprinted the godly values of diligence, integrity, and love upon my malleable heart. I appreciate you dearly; may your gentle soul continue to rest in peace, "Bami."

The second father on the row is Reverend Israel Odedele, who midwifed me into Christendom. He painstakingly sacrificed his time and resources to pour into a young teenager whose future was bleak and uncertain. He thoroughly discipled me to stand on my feet as a Christian. I am very grateful, sir.

The third father on the row is Late Venerable Ibukun Wale Falope; I fondly called him "my Dah." A remarkable and excellent man indeed, "my dah" was the definition of a perfect gentleman for me. A very genuine, well-read, well-exposed, godly man with a deep-seated hunger to know God and His Word. He would often wake me up to pray and study the Bible with him while preparing for his ministrations. Little did he know that he was raising another instrument for God to use. He simply gave me his shoulder to stand on so I could see the world farther and better. My dah, I love you deeply; keep resting in the bosom of the Lord until we meet again. Your legacy will never be forgotten.

Finally, my spiritual father and mentor, Pastor Toye Ademola. He is the man who birthed me into the pastoral ministry. Out of ignorance, I have done everything possible to run away from the call of God, but in due time, God brought me under his tutelage, and he did an excellent job at unveiling the mask for me.

He is a spiritual father worthy of emulation in every sense, and the most fascinating thing for me is that he does not just teach me the Word; he does the work; he leaves a pattern for ministry without misery for me to follow.

His interest in seeing me fulfill my destiny is unprecedented, and I am deeply grateful. My prayer is always that his labor over me will never be in vain; thank you so much, sir.

I appreciate my four boys (the Generals), the mighty seeds of the righteous man; I am enlisted in the school of fatherhood because God gave you to me; your support and sacrifices are highly valued.

Introduction

I must confess that I did not embark on the project of writing this book to display my prolific writing skills, nor was the reward of an additional source of income my motivation.

It all started with a conversation with my sister, who went to Prison Evangelism. She was busy expressing her pain over the number of young men locked behind bars in the United States. As the conversation proceeded, it occurred to me that her story was just one side of the coin; there are so many other young men who are free, but no better than the ones behind bars.

Their confusion about their own identity and their inability to solve life's daily challenges as young fathers keep them mentally confined.

My sister and I discussed my frustration with those mentally imprisoned. We both asked ourselves, what can we do to help a society that is declining in values and failing at raising responsible sons who will become responsible fathers? My sister answers our monotonous question and says, "My brother, it's time for fathers to arise."

That response stayed with me for days as I continued meditating: Fathers, Arise!

In my meditation, it occurred to me that there is no manual for fatherhood, as everyone picks up things from the ones we find around, who are not in any way aware of their influence on the tender and malleable minds around them; so, there is no intentionality in their actions.

This urgent need birthed the desire to embark on this divine project. I must also state clearly that I am not embarking on this assignment as an expert father who is here to dish it out to others. Fatherhood is not for perfect men; it is a journey for imperfect men to come to perfection, and we are all on it together as we learn along.

The intrinsic purpose of all men is fatherhood. God designed men to fulfill the role of a father in the lives of those around them. Dr. Myles Munroe says, "Although every man is called to be a father, knowing how to live for this purpose is not automatic."

Men must understand and master the notable traits of fatherhood. They fulfill the position and role they were created for by exhibiting leadership, integrity, responsibility, and obedience to the ultimate Father of fathers, our Father God in heaven.

God intends that everything He does with us will not end with us. God is eternal, and His work must be perpetuated through us, which is called legacy. *No wonder the Psalmist says one generation shall praise your name unto another* - **Psalm 145:4.**

The greatest crisis in national development is not a lack of funds or investment. Behavioral scientists have proven that the greatest crisis in any nation is the lack of fathers.

Also, former U.S. Attorney General William Barr said, 'If you look at the one factor that most closely correlates with crime, it's not poverty, it's not unemployment, it's not lack of education; it's the father's absence in the family.

The scarcity of fathers threatens human existence more than all the world-power nuclear weapons put together.

Fatherhood isn't about ownership; it's about stewardship. God has given your children to you on a lease with an expiration date.

Your first assignment is to provide love to make the children feel secure, values to set boundaries and make them wise, light to walk in, and a lifestyle to follow.

Your next assignment is to prepare them to go out into the world and put into practice the things you've taught them. As a father, you are the bow that sends your children as living arrows into the world.

So, you must do these two assignments so well that when the time comes, you can confidently release them, celebrate your investment, mentor them, pray for them, and watch them blossom and flourish as responsible fathers.

Fatherhood is one of the most challenging tasks anybody could have, unfortunately, there is no manual for the job; we have to learn on the job.

> *"We are not made wise by the recollection of our past, but by the responsibility for our future,"*
> **- George Bernard Shaw.**

In the quote above, George Bernard Shaw is teaching us as fathers that there is no wisdom in blaming past fathers for our societal failure; however, wisdom lies in taking responsibility to shape future fathers so that the errors of the past will not be propagated in the future.

As a father, you might not have been privileged to be raised by someone who has modeled God - the Father of all fathers to you. That might have justified the errors you have committed thus far, but it won't be acceptable anymore.

This book is written to wake your consciousness to the father you ought to be - a model of God and to call you to arise and salvage the pending ruin of the next generation.

I strongly recommend this book for every father, young and old. Whether you are at a crossroads in your fatherhood journey or doing fine but desire to see more fathers like you populate our world. The stories, proverbs, Bible references, and the father's prayers captured in this book will never leave you the same.

There is obviously no time any longer. Why should we wait any further? It's time, Fathers, Arise!

CHAPTER 1

Redefining Fatherhood?

> *"A good father is one of the most unsung, unpraised, unnoticed, and yet one of the most valuable assets in our society."*
> **- Billy Graham.**

Due to my God-given assignment, I have been privileged to counsel several young men battling emotional issues. One common denominator I have noticed is that the root cause of their challenge is an emotional wound caused by their fathers. Despite their growth over the years, they rarely discuss the wound, and even more rarely heal it; the wound persists.

Fatherhood can make or break a child, and the positive or negative impact can linger for ages.

The advancement of technology has heightened the demand for fatherhood in the 21st century, constant cultural shifts, and the irrepressible pull of the economic demands to raise a decent family. If you're a father, you might be fighting many battles - for your marriage, family, and even your heart. And securing the tenacity to keep fighting every day is never an easy task.

Being a father is a complex journey encompassing love, discipline, responsibility, and growth. It's a story that unfolds throughout a man's life and is unique to each individual.

Fatherhood transcends blood ties and duty; it's a steadfast commitment to love, guide, and support, regardless of challenges.

"Sometimes, a father may not be the one who gives you your genes; he may just be the one who gives you his heart.

> *"When a father gives to his son, both laugh; when a son gives to his father, both cry."*
> **- William Shakespeare.**

Over the years, we have used the words "Dad" and "Father" interchangeably. Even though they both refer to a male parent, there's a subtle difference between the two:

A father is a more formal term. It emphasizes the biological or legal connection to the child. You might use it when referring to someone else's father, in official documents, or in a more serious context.

A dad is a more casual term. It suggests a closer, more affectionate relationship. You would typically use "dad" to refer to your own father or when speaking to a child about their father.

Here's an analogy: Think of "father" as your last name; everyone has one, and "dad" as your nickname; it's more personal.

From the explanation above, every dad should be a father, but not all fathers can be called a dad.

For consistency in this book, we will stick to the word "father."

Obviously, a father's presence increases a child's chances of confidence, strength, and success in life.

There are no substitutes for a father; no teacher, guardian, or friend can be a father.

A thousand teachers cannot replace a father.

Robert L. Backman says, *"Father is the noblest title a man can be given. It is more than a biological role. It signifies a patriarch, a leader, an exemplar, a confidant, a teacher, a hero, a friend."*

The world has given the sacred office of fatherhood several names and definitions, which vary among tribes and tongues, countries, colors, ages, and grades.

So, who is a father?

- A father is a male parent who has a child or children. This is the biological father of a child.

- Fathers can also be the men who raise children, even if they are not the biological father. This could be a stepfather, adoptive father, or foster father.

- A father can also be a title for a priest, monk, or other religious leader, especially in Christianity.

- A father can also refer to the founder or originator of something, like "the father of modern medicine."

C.S. Lewis says, "I believe in Christianity as I believe that the Sun has risen not only because I see it but because by it, I see everything else."

In line with the quote above, I see the world through the eye of the Word of God (the Bible), which is God's documented words; so, I see everything in life through the lens of God's infallible Word.

Therefore, my definition of who a father is will be according to the Word of God.

> *"For though you might have ten thousand instructors in Christ, yet you do not have many fathers; for in Christ Jesus, I have begotten you through the gospel. [16] Therefore, I urge you to imitate me,"*
> *- 1 Corinthians 4:15-16 NKJV.*

- **A father is a person who is present, observable, and you can imitate.**

He is the one who tells you, "Do what I do, say what I say, dress like me, go to where I go, just be like me.

Any man can be a teacher, but it takes a treasure to be a father.

A teacher teaches you with words and the help of other teaching aids, but a father teaches you with his life.

Since life does not come with a manual, any son who lacks the template of a father will eventually be misinformed, and these misinformed sons always turn out deformed.

Take note: Your son might disregard your advice, but be assured that he will imitate your example, regardless of your behavior.

Actions speak louder than words; you don't need to tell your son how to live; live, and he will pick who you are.

The lessons that sons learn from their fathers are often not what they intentionally teach; they are little wisdom nuggets gleaned at unsuspecting moments, and that little wisdom forms them.

A good example is Eliezer, the Chief Servant of Abraham

Then he said, "O LORD God of my master Abraham, please give me success this day, and show kindness to my master Abraham." - Genesis 24:12 NKJV.

Eliezer has observed Abraham's lifestyle over the years and concluded that his God could also be trusted for his success.

There was never a time when Abraham sermonized him; Abraham maintained a lifestyle that depended on God absolutely, and the members of his household emulated him.

According to the Bible, a father is called Abba—a Hebrew word that means source, sustainer, progenitor (supporter of the gene), foundation, and root.

- **A father is the source, sustainer, progenitor, and root of his children.**

If a father is the root, it is practically impossible to grow well if you are disconnected from him. You keep looking up to a father no matter how tall you grow.

Pope John XXIII says, "It is easier for fathers to have children than for children to have a real father."

This acronym for father seems to communicate it well:

- **F**aithfully
- **A**ligning
- **T**he
- **H**ome to
- **E**ternal
- **R**ealities

Fathers are heavenly treasures that perpetuate eternal realities and enhance life's worth; they are not easy to come by.

> *"By profession, I am a soldier and take great pride in that fact, but I am also infinitely prouder to be a father. A soldier destroys in order to build; the father only builds, never destroys."*
> *- General Douglas MacArthur.*

Suppose we want to impact the next generation positively. In that case, we must bless them by telling them about God's promises, principles, and purposes and how we can preserve the earth by raising sons and daughters who will manifest God's glory in this dark and perverse world. When we do that, we'll see true transformation in our families and a positive shift in our culture and communities as we align them to eternal realities.

The Father's Day Celebration:

According to the article: A Brief History of Father's Day by Brett & Kate McKay, published in The Art of Manliness on May 30, 2021, updated on September 3, 2021.

There are two stories about what birthed the Father's Day Celebration.

The first story is about Sonora Smart Dodd, who decided to honor her father, William Smart. The Civil War veteran, William Smart, became a widower when his wife died giving birth to their sixth child. He raised the six children by himself on their small farm in Washington. To show her appreciation for all the hard work and love William gave her and her siblings, Sonora thought there should be a day to pay homage to him and other dads like him. She initiated the Father's Day Celebration on June 19, 1910, the third Sunday in June.

The second story around the first Father's Day Celebration in America was the case of Grace Golden Clayton, a minister of the local Methodist church in Fairmont, West Virginia, on July 5, 1908, proposing to hold service to celebrate fathers after a deadly mine explosion that killed 361 men.

However, in 1972, during President Nixon's administration, the U.S. officially recognized Father's Day as a national holiday.

No matter which side of the story we believe, the common ground for all is that our fathers are worth celebrating, as they give of themselves to see the next generation rise.

Different nations have chosen different days to celebrate fathers over the years, as they deserve much more.

Here is a list of dates when countries celebrate Father's Day.

- March 14–Iran.

- March 19–Bolivia, Honduras, Italy, Lichtenstein, Portugal, Spain.

- May 8–South Korea.

- First Sunday in June–Lithuania.

- Second Sunday in June–Austria, Ecuador, Belgium.

- Third Sunday in June–The United States, Antigua, Bahamas, Bangladesh, Bulgaria, Canada, Chile, Columbia, Costa Rica, Cuba, Cyprus, Czech Republic, France, Greece, Guyana, Hong Kong, India, Ireland, Jamaica, Japan, Malaysia, Malta, Mauritius, Mexico, Netherlands, Pakistan, Panama, Paraguay, Peru, Philippines, Puerto Rico, Saint Vincent, Singapore, Slovakia, South Africa, Sri Lanka, Switzerland, Trinidad, Turkey, United Kingdom, Venezuela, Zimbabwe.

- June 17–El Salvador, Guatemala.

- June 23–Nicaragua, Poland, and Uganda.

- Second Sunday in July–Uruguay.

- Last Sunday in July–Dominican Republic.

- Second Sunday in August–Brazil.

- August 8–Taiwan, China.

- August 24–Argentina.

- First Sunday in September–Australia, New Zealand.

- New Moon of September–Nepal.

- First Sunday in October–Luxembourg.

- Second Sunday in November–Estonia, Finland, Norway, Sweden.

- December 5–Thailand.

If you are privileged to read this book and your country is yet to assign a date to celebrate fathers (*although fathers are heroes to be celebrated daily*), may I implore you to start your rising as fathers by requesting your government to do something about it? If we don't acknowledge and appreciate what fathers have done, future fathers will have less motivation to make the sacrifices of fatherhood and strive for excellence.

A supportive community is essential, and community support is key to encouraging fathers to step up. This includes encouraging open dialogues about fatherhood, providing resources for parenting education, and facilitating connections among fathers. Community programs that offer mentorship, workshops, and support groups can help fathers navigate the complexities of parenting. By sharing experiences and insights, fathers can build a network of support that reinforces their commitment to being actively involved in their children's lives.

I got the story below from a beloved brother that we met on one of the online platforms; the story underscores the much-needed reason fathers should be celebrated; please enjoy the read and learn.

"I grew up in a home where I had an idea of the father being a provider (finance and leadership-wise), but I didn't learn early enough what the father had to go through to provide for his family.

Some 15 years ago, while my father was still working with the Nigerian Embassy in Rome, I went to his office to get money for a train ticket. A friend had told me about an opening in his city, 5 hours away from ours, so I needed some money to get on the fast train.

His colleague and friend saw me when I came in and asked me to wait in his office as my dad was in a meeting. When I told the colleague about the urgency of my train leaving in an hour, he went to the meeting arena and found a way to signal him that I was around. I saw the rush as he walked towards me. I told him why I was in his office, and he brought out an envelope to give me the money I needed. Suddenly, his friend's office door was pushed open, and I heard this loud voice. Good morning, sir. At that point, it was his boss, the head of chancery, a very young man. He spoke to him in a very rude manner. I've never witnessed anyone talk to him in such a manner.

Dad responded: Yes, Sir.

The Boss: How dare you keep me waiting? Are you normal?

Dad responded: I am very sorry, Sir. "I better not get to that hall before you……." and the semi-illiterate, poor diction, ill-mannered young man with a harsh ……. accent hurled insults at my dad while he stood at attention.

Without looking at me, my dad said, Son, can your trip wait till tomorrow?

Seeing my dad, someone with highly successful younger siblings who bow and prostrate to greet him in that state, broke me. My journey back home was tormenting and depressing.

Later in life, when I became a father, I realized that the King must submit outside his Kingdom to bring bread to the table.

This post is not about my dad, for the old man has retired and is enjoying his retirement. This post is about the father - King and Commoner — and an awakening in the hearts of those he fights for. The only place in the world where a father is truly a king is his home. As soon as he steps out in search of daily bread, he automatically becomes a commoner; he begs, weeps, is insulted, sometimes humiliated, and humbled. He kneels before lesser men and is demeaned by **clients, superiors, customers, employers, etc.**

He takes all these with pride, even though he feels undignified, knowing that it is in his submission that bread is guaranteed at his family's table. He knows that submission is the survivor's apparatus in the harsh economic world.

When labor is over, he picks himself up, adorning his **kingly robes**, and returns to his home, where his honor resides. When he returns, and if he returns, those in his home must help remind him that here is his kingdom where he reigns supreme as Husband, Father, and King!

To the fathers paying the price for the greatness of the next generation, I salute you!!

You don't have to break the bank to honor your father; as little as a note expressing your most profound gratitude for some of the things you love and admire about him, especially his sacrifices to see you rise, will go a long way. Just tell him you're glad to be his son or daughter because many of our fathers secretly nurse the wound of inadequacy and regret.

TIME FOR REflECTION

1. What do you find most captivating in this chapter?

____

____

____

____

2. Based on the new insights gained, what commitment(s) will you make?

____

____

____

____

3. What are your action steps to implement your commitment(s)?

____

____

____

____

Fatherhood Diversity

> *"My father always provided me a safe place to land and a hard place from which to launch."*
> *- Chelsea Clinton.*

Historically, society viewed fathers primarily as providers or authority figures. However, contemporary society is acknowledging the importance of emotional availability and nurturing in fatherhood. Society now encourages modern fathers to embrace vulnerability, express emotions, and build strong, open relationships with their children. This shift in perspective benefits children and allows fathers to experience deeper connections with their families, redefining what it means to be a man in today's world.

In this chapter, we will attempt to classify fathers based on research by human psychologists.

Fathers can be classified by how they give love and discipline to their children.

There are typically four types of fathers we could get from these perspectives:

1. **Permissive Father**—A permissive father loves a child all the time without discipline. He acts more as a friend than as a father.

He is often on **reserved duty** and treats fatherhood like a part-time job. He's engaged with his children, but only occasionally, maybe only on the weekends when it's most convenient for him. He has good intentions, but his children require more time than he's willing or able to give. His children need him to be a full-time father, but he's content with giving them a part-time effort.

It must be clear to all that as much as your children want your presents (gifts), they need your presence much more; be there!

Living in an era where we are taking everything online must not deceive us into taking our fatherhood tasks online; Fatherhood is not a task that can be accomplished online. Knowing that the father is at home sets a boundary for some childish naughtiness and invokes an uncommon sense of safety for the family.

A permissive father is lenient and tolerant of his children's behavior. He often sets rules or limits and allows his children to make decisions with minimal guidance or supervision.

Characteristics of a Permissive Father:

- **Loose discipline**: He rarely punishes or disciplines his children, even for negative behavior. Always remember that whatever you permit persists.

- **Minimal boundaries**: He sets a few rules or limits, allowing his children to do as they please. Children left without boundaries will eventually become wild.

- **Kid-glove treatment**: He is often too lenient and forgiving, even when his children make mistakes and deserve discipline.

- **Lack of structure**: He may not provide enough structure or routine in his children's lives.

Potential Consequences of Having a Permissive Father:

- **Behavioral problems**: Children raised by permissive fathers may develop behavioral problems, such as aggression, impulsiveness, or substance abuse.

- **Lack of self-discipline**: They may struggle with self-discipline and responsibility. Since there are no boundaries, there will be little or nothing to restrain and sound an alarm—excess!

- **Academic difficulties**: They may have trouble in school due to a lack of focus and motivation. Obviously, without clearly set boundaries for timing, the right time will be spent on the wrong things, yielding little or no positive outcome.

- **Emotional immaturity**: They may have difficulty managing their emotions and forming healthy relationships. As social beings, every child should be instructed in the rules of engagement in the social space; the inability to do that will breed a disconnected child.

2. **Detached Father**–A detached father adopts the style of NO LOVE, NO DISCIPLINE; the child is on his or her own. He may have helped bring them into the world, but he doesn't want to have anything to do with them. He's so engaged in his world, and the children seem to be unnecessary interruptions and distractions. The children see him, but they can't talk to him. He comes home and secludes himself from the family. He may not be a terrible father. He's just emotionally detached from others in his home. So, he struggles in silence as his family also struggles with his emotional absence. An uninvolved father is emotionally distant and shows little or no interest in his children's lives. He may be physically present, but he's often preoccupied with other things and does not actively participate in his children's activities or development. This lack of interest often stems from a distraction from work or extra-marital affairs, or from getting back at the spouse after an unresolved conflict. But it ought not to be, as the children never forced themselves upon us; we brought them forth.

Characteristics of a Detached Father:

- **Emotional detachment**: He is emotionally distant and does not show much affection or support for his children.

- **Lack of interest**: He is not interested in his children's lives or activities.

- **Minimal involvement**: He is rarely involved in his children's upbringing or development.

- **Preoccupied with other things**: He is often preoccupied with work, hobbies, or other interests.

Potential Consequences of Having a Detached Father:

- **Emotional problems**: Children raised by uninvolved fathers may experience emotional problems such as low self-esteem, anxiety, or depression.

- **Behavioral problems**: They may develop behavioral problems, such as aggression, delinquency, or substance abuse.

- **Academic difficulties**: They may have trouble in school due to a lack of motivation or support.

- **Relationship problems**: They may have difficulty forming healthy relationships in adulthood.

3. **Dictatorial Father**—A dictatorial father adopts a style of disciplining a child all the time, without any love. He is not disengaged, but he's enraged most of the time. He always seems angry with his children, and because of that anger, he hurts others with his words, tone, and actions.

   A dictatorial father is strict, demanding, and controlling. He may use punishment to enforce his authority and may be unwilling to listen to his children's opinions or feelings.

   Dictatorial fathers are often less nurturing and affectionate and have high expectations with limited flexibility. They may also have "children should be seen and not heard" approach.

He is the lion in his family, constantly roaring, so everybody tiptoes around the home when he's around.

Characteristics of a Dictatorial Father:

- **Strict discipline**: He uses punishments, such as spanking or time-outs, to enforce his rules.

- **High expectations**: He sets high expectations for his children and expects them to meet them.

- **Controlling behavior**: He is controlling and does not allow his children much autonomy.

- **Lack of communication**: He may not be open to communication or feedback from his children.

Potential Consequences of Having a Dictatorial Father:

- **Low self-esteem**: Children raised by authoritarian parents may have low self-esteem due to a lack of positive reinforcement.

- **Anxiety and depression**: They may experience anxiety or depression due to the constant pressure to conform.

- **Behavioral problems**: They may develop behavioral problems, such as aggression or delinquency, to rebel against their parents' control.

- **Difficulty forming relationships**: They may have difficulty forming healthy relationships in adulthood due to a lack of trust or emotional intimacy.

4. **Balanced Father**–A balanced father adopts a delicate blend of love and discipline.

   He balances clear rules and limits with a caring and understanding perspective. Balanced fathers are nurturing, responsive, and supportive, but also set clear boundaries for their children. They try to control children's behavior by explaining rules, discussing, and reasoning, and they listen to their children's viewpoints. A balanced father will endeavor to model the responsible adult he desires his children to grow into, and he expects his children to behave in a mature, independent, and age-appropriate way. He loves, protects, serves, and provides for their physical, emotional, and spiritual needs. He's not afraid to affirm his love for his children; they feel emotionally and physically safe and secure when in his presence. Based on the available statistics, the balanced father is declared the best type of father. A balanced father combines elements of permissive, detached, and dictatorial types of fathering in a way that is both supportive and demanding. He sets clear expectations while responding to his children's needs and feelings. He provides guidance and support while allowing his children to develop their independence.

Characteristics of a Balanced Father:

- **Clear expectations**: He sets clear expectations for his children and consistently enforces them.

- **Supportive and encouraging:** He supports and encourages his children's efforts.

- **Open communication**: He is open to communication and feedback from his children.

- **Respectful of boundaries**: He respects his children's boundaries and allows them to make their own decisions.

- **Provides guidance and support:** He provides guidance and support when needed, while allowing his children to develop their independence.

Potential Benefits of Having a Balanced Father:

- **Positive self-esteem**: Children raised by balanced parents may have higher self-esteem because of the sense of security and support they enjoy.

- **Strong relationships**: They may have stronger relationships with their parents and peers.

- **Academic success**: They may be more likely to succeed in school because of their motivation and self-discipline.

- **Healthy development**: They may develop into well-adjusted, independent adults.

Note: We can see from these different types of fathers that permissive, detached, and dictatorial fathers can have negative consequences; while a balanced father is often considered the most effective approach, it's important to remember that raising children is more complex than it looks, and many factors influence it. There is no one-size-fits-all approach to raising children; depending on their different circumstances and uniqueness, what works best for one family may not work for another.

While discussing types of fathers, I would like to share the article below with you for more enlightenment. Consider this fictional for educational purposes only.

It was an experience of a medical doctor with his patient and the father. The father came in with his son to the doctor's office. One could easily mistake them for twin brothers, aside the fact that the father was bigger and appeared older. The boy had a feature of adolescents' rapid growth. Adolescents are people between 10 and 19 years old. The boy who was the patient was 16. Many things are unique about people in this age group. A key aspect is their outlook on life. They strongly believe in fairy tales. Don't mind me; I was also once in the same dreamland before age, and the reality of life woke me up.

What can I do for you during this visit, Julius, the doctor asked. My father promised me a dental braces for my examination success.

The patient responded, I had just passed and was here to get my braces.

They had gone to a dental unit of the hospital earlier, and a staff directed them back to the general outpatient department for a referral. So, Julius (the patient) was in the doctor's office to get a referral letter from the dentist for his dental braces, which his father promised him as a reward for success in his exam.

The doctor wanted to know his reason for wanting dental braces, so he asked if he had any tooth anomalies. The doctor was shocked at the answer Julius gave him, and this is what prompted the writing of this piece.

Julius replied to the doctor that the celebrity he loved was using a dental brace, which was why he wanted one. Julius' response came as a shock to the doctor. As a general practitioner, I know people use dental braces for cosmetic reasons. Still, a 16 years old boy with no teeth anomalies wanted a dental brace because the hero celebrity he was watching on TV was using it. This shock made the doctor turn to the father, who had granted such a request. A bigger shock came from the father. Did you hear your son's reason for getting a dental brace, the doctor asked Julius's father. He said yes and further justified it by saying, "Doctor, what can I do? He said that was what he wanted as a reward for his exam's success".

"Even at home, that is how he behaves. If he does not get what he wants, he becomes unhappy." The father said with a worrisome look.
"A 16-year-old boy dictates what he wants for you at home, and you, as a father, will always condone that?" the doctor says, while the father smiles back sheepishly.

The doctor saw this situation as a concern and immediately switched to counseling mode. This is an impending danger here; a young man's future is at stake. This is a case of wrong parenting for an adolescent.

The doctor asked Julius for permission to counsel him and his father together. He did not decline, although he wondered what the counseling was for. Any problem? Julius asked.

The counseling format has always been basically to ask what the patients know about the topic, and the counselor gives them all the correct information and options and then guides them to make a rational decision that is best for them. The doctor ventured out on this counseling assignment, dealing with **adolescence and parenting.**

He asked Julius what he understood by being an adolescent. He seemed not to understand much about adolescence, despite being one. The doctor also asked the father about parenting an adolescent, and he said, is there anything special about parenting adolescents?

This ignorance is why Julius and the father were at the doctor's office at such a time for a cosmetic dental brace, motivated by a hero celebrity.

These tips about adolescence may be helpful.

1. Adolescence is a stage of life for people between 10 and 19 years.

2. This stage can be developmentally divided into three phases , according to the World Health Organization (WHO):

   o **Early adolescence (10-13) -** Early adolescents have the brain of a child and an adult's body.

   o **Mid-adolescence (14-16)–**Mid-adolescence has 50% of a child's brain and 50% of an adult's brain with the body of an adult.

o **Late adolescence (17-19) -** Late adolescents have the brain of an adult and the body of an adult.

Adolescents' decisions at each stage of life go hand-in-hand with their peculiarities. Julius was 16. He has the body of an adult already, but 50% of a child's brain. Is this not obvious from the decision made?

Now to parenting, parenting is guiding and nurturing a child in all aspects of life, whether you are a biological or nonbiological parent. You can parent a child in four ways, and the meaning of each parenting style is based on two issues: **love and discipline**, as we can see above.

The doctor then turned to Julius's father: which type of father do you think you have been? The 60-year-old man was quiet for almost 2 minutes; surprisingly, with tears rolling down his cheeks, he said, "Doctor, I never knew about all these types and their consequences as you explained. Undoubtedly, the permissive parenting style seems to be the one I have been using with Julius." "Doctor, what can l do now? Is it not too late for him? That was how l raised his two elder brothers. It is saddening to know that they have also not turned out well. The first brother had a drug issue, and the second brother was irresponsible."

Amazingly, Julius, in tears after hearing the doctor's unsolicited counsel and education on **adolescence**, **parenting**, and its consequences, and listening to his father's helpless question said, "Daddy, it is not too late. I don't want any dental braces again. Daddy, authoritatively guide me. The best way that will make me turn out best.

The two hugged each other in the river of tears and walked out of the doctor's office.

The words of Prophet Hosea readily comes to mind at a time like this: "My people are destroyed for lack of knowledge…" **Hosea 4:6 NKJV**

This doctor is genuinely a hero; he has just saved a life, a future, a family, and a generation.

This flawed approach, if followed by Julius and subsequent generations, would have resulted in a devastating, multigenerational problem.

This is the heart of this book: to wake the consciousness of fathers to what is at stake and to address the rising need to salvage the next generation from impending doom.

Every father reading this anywhere in the world, loving a child without disciplining them is not loving them; it is destroying their lives.

The Bible admonishes us on correction and discipline in the verses below:

> *"If you withhold correction and punishment from your children, you demonstrate a lack of true love. So, prove your love and be prompt to punish them"*
> *- Proverbs 13:24 TPT.*

Please note that delayed discipline is affirmed foolishness.

> *"Correction and discipline are good for children. If they have their way, they will make their mothers ashamed of them"*
> *- Proverbs 29:15 GNT.*

> *"Discipline your son, and he will give you happiness and peace of mind"*
> *- Proverbs 29:17 TLB.*
>
> *"Children do foolish things, but if you punish them, they will learn not to do them"*
> *- Proverbs 22:15 ERV*
>
> *"Don't be afraid to correct your young ones; a spanking won't kill them. A good spanking, in fact, might save them from something worse than death"*
> *- Proverbs 23:13-14 MSG.*

Below is the extract from Proverbs 13:24 Believer's Bible Commentary:

To withhold punishment from a child when it is deserved is to encourage the child in sin and thus contribute to his eventual ruin.

The parent who spares his rod might think he is manifesting love, but God says it is hatred.

For years, Dr. Benjamin Spock encouraged parents to be permissive. After seeing a generation of bratty, pesky children, he admitted that he had been wrong. He says, "Inability to be firm is, to my mind, the commonest problem of parents in America today."

He placed some parts of the blame on the experts- "the child psychiatrists, psychologists, teachers, social workers, and pediatricians, like himself."

The parent who genuinely loves their child does not condone naughtiness but disciplines the child promptly.

A good strategy is to make sure that any discipline you give to your child also makes them a better person.

Consider this: if you want to discipline inappropriate behavior, you can free two birds with one key by making the discipline practical. Like the sports coach who makes players do push-ups if they don't meet a standard. Next time your child acts out, take a moment and think of a discipline that can help develop their character.

It could be something as simple as cleaning the bathroom or memorizing capital cities. If you want something bigger, try volunteer work or ask them to help paint the house. They may not like it, but that's the point. When they grow up, they'll thank you for building their character and preparing them for real life.

Please love your children, meet their needs, cater to them, ask for their opinions, and respect their views if they benefit their present and future. However, make sure that after putting everything together and considering their highest good, you have the final say by showing them the right path.

They may not appreciate your parenting type as a father today, but don't worry, as you keep a balance between love and discipline, they will look back tomorrow as fulfilled souls, and they will forget the pain of discipline because of the magnitude of its gains; they will bless God for you as their guide through life.

TIME FOR REflECTION

1. What do you find most captivating in this chapter?

____

____

____

____

2. Based on the new insights gained, what commitment(s) will you make?

____

____

____

____

3. What are your action steps to implement your commitment(s)?

____

____

____

____

CHAPTER 3

Asset or Liability Father?

> *"A father is someone you look up to no matter how tall you grow."*
> **- Unknown.**

Taking a clue from the previous chapters, it is agreed that fathers are irreplaceable treasures, and they come in diverse variations, as diverse as our beliefs, temperaments, and social and cultural backgrounds.

Whether your father was a tough man, a simple man, or in-between, there's no question that your father has shaped your worldview and influenced your thinking process.

Even though fatherhood is not about cloning your children, it is about being a leading light that will help them see who they are within and their connecting points to their world for maximum relevance and exploits.

Every child deserves a father who will model God the Father, before them, teach them the truth of God's Word, and show them how to receive the gift of eternal life. You may not have had a great father as a role model, but you can change that today by becoming a great father yourself. Your family could begin this beautiful tradition as you give your life to Jesus Christ.

Author and Bible teacher Gordon MacDonald tells the story of three medieval stonemasons working on a building project when a passer-by asked them what they were doing. The first replied that he was laying bricks. The second described his work as that of building a wall. But the third stonemason showed genuine esteem for his work when he says, "I'm building a great cathedral."

If you present this same question to any two fathers concerning their role in the family, you can get the same contrast. The first may says, "I'm supporting a family," but the second may see things differently and says, "I'm raising exceptional children." The former looks at his job as putting bread on the table, but the latter sees things from God's perspective: he is taking part in shaping lives.

The great Bible teacher R.A. Torrey once says, 'A man's success as a Christian leader cannot be determined until one sees his grandchildren.'

Reflecting on our childhoods, we often wish our fathers had acted differently in certain situations. But the most important thing is to prevent our past from having a detrimental effect on how we parent and connect with our children.

In my daily quest to know God more through His holy, infallible word called the Bible, the patterns of fathers captured in the Bible leave us with two major types. These types are not directly stated in the Bible, but I have safely inferred them for learning purposes.

Types of Fathers:

1. Liability Fathers

A liability is a person or thing whose presence or behavior is likely to embarrass or put one at a disadvantage.

So, who is a **liability father?**

A **liability father** is a father whose name and life negatively affect his family and place them at a disadvantage. Liability fathers have the following characteristics:

- **They have names that spell disfavor and invoke dishonor.** For example, Prophet Eli. Any of his descendants, no matter how innocent they were, would lack the favor and honor of God because of how he handled the priesthood and his sons. Biblical references—**1 Samuel 3:18; 1 Samuel 2:30-33 & 1 King 2:26-27.**

- **They are boastful, which hampers their descendants' future peace.** For example, King Hezekiah pridefully showed all his treasure to the Babylonian ambassadors, leading to his descendants' entering captivity—**2 Kings 20:15-18.**

- **They are selfish fathers who only consider what benefits them now.** For example, King Hezekiah pleaded for his health recovery and did not bother to beg for forgiveness for his prideful act since the consequences would not affect him but his descendants**—2 Kings 20:15-19; Isaiah 39:6-8.**

- **They are not generational thinkers; they only live for the present.** They lack self-control and cannot delay gratification. These fathers could take a thousand dollars today for their enjoyment rather than delaying gratification so that their descendants could receive a million dollars in the future. For example, Esau gave away his birthright as the first son just because of his untamed appetite for food. Esau's descendants would have been the beneficiaries of Abraham's covenant blessings. Esau says, "What is the birthright to me?"–**Genesis 25:29-34.**

- **They harm others with their words and decisions in the long run.** Unfortunately, when God sent the young Prophet Samuel to the older Prophet Eli to point out his errors and reveal God's verdicts, Prophet Eli replies loosely, "He is God; let Him do whatever He wants." Those nonchalant statements and decisions delisted the entire generation of Prophet Eli from the honorable class of Priesthood and plunged them into a curse of untimely death and a life of embarrassment–**1 Samuel 3:16-18; 1 Samuel 2:33.**

- **They create problems for their posterity to solve.** Knowing that every unconquered territory becomes a slippery ground for the next generation is vital. For example, King Saul disobeyed God by refusing to destroy the Amalekites completely and conquer them once and for all. Unfortunately, Haman, the descendant of the Amalekites who was an official in the palace of King Ahasuerus at Shushan, woke up one day with a desire to annihilate the descendants of King Saul and the entire Jewish race. So, King Saul's disobedience became a liability for his family down the line - **1 Samuel 15:18-19; Esther 3:1, 6 &13.**

- **The behavior of a liability father leaves a curse for the next generation instead of blessings.** An excellent example of a liability father who shows this characteristic is Joab. He was a commander of the army of Israel under the kingship of King David. Joab was a fearless and powerful soldier, but he was unforgiving and very vindictive. These unhealthy traits that he did not deal with incurred a generational curse of bloody death that afflicted him and his family–**1 Kings 2:30-33.**
Also, Prophet Gehazi's greed made him a liability father, as he left the burden of an incurable disease, leprosy, for his innocent family to bear–**2 Kings 5:27.**

- **They leave debts for their families to pay instead of an inheritance.** Unfortunately, some fathers do not want to be liability fathers, but their wrong financial choices and decisions put them in this group. A good example was the prophet stated in 2 Kings 4:1-3. The sons knew nothing about his financial transactions, but they were on the verge of becoming slaves just because of their father's liabilities. Had it not been for Prophet Elisha's intervention, the destiny of those sons and the wife would have ended in shame and regret.

2. **Asset Fathers**: The second type of father is an **asset father**. An asset is a useful or valuable thing, person, or quality.
So, who is an **Asset Father?**
An Asset Father is a father with a valuable name whose life positively impacts his family and places them at an unusual advantage. Asset Fathers have the following characteristics:
They are people who keep their commitment.

This commitment opens doors of opportunity for their families. Jonathan's commitment to his friendship with King David opened the door of opportunity for his grandson, Mephibosheth, to live all his life at the king's expense - **2 Samuel 9:6-7.**

- **They are not selfish but generational thinkers (future-minded).** Barzillai was a wealthy man who showed kindness to King David while in exile because of Absalom's forceful takeover of his kingdom. Afterwards, when King David returned to his throne and wanted to bless Barzillai, Barzillai recommended his sons for the reward instead because he had a short time left to live compared to his sons, who could enjoy it for a longer time. King David blessed the sons of Barzillai in -**1 Kings 2:7** because of the kindness of their father.

- **They strategically invest in relationships that could yield dividends to their posterity.** Hanun showed kindness to King David, and King David showed kindness to his son, too - **2 Samuel 10:2.**

  Also, the Kenites showed kindness to the Israelites when they came out of Egypt, and many years after, King Saul remembered their descendants and spared their lives when they were about to war with their nation—**1 Samuel 15:6.**

- **Asset Fathers have names that are collateral.** King Solomon lost face with God, and God prepared to take the kingdom away entirely from him. But God could not do that because of the obedience of his father, King David, which was like a collateral - **1 Kings 11:34.**

- **They leave a tangible and intangible inheritance for their posterity.** Abraham had a covenant with God that passed on the blessings of the covenant to his descendants. **Genesis 25:5; Genesis 26:4-5.**

Below is a story of a contemporary example of an **Asset Father**, a piece that I got from *"The Word for Today."* Whether every detail is factual or not, it carries a powerful message worth reflecting on. Indeed, what goes around comes around.

In the late nineteenth century, a member of Parliament went to Scotland to make an important speech. He traveled to Edinburgh by train, then took a horse-drawn carriage southward to his destination. But the roads were terrible, and the carriage became mired in mud. A Scottish farm boy came to the rescue of the horse team and helped pull the carriage loose. The Member of Parliament asked the boy how much he owed him. "Nothing," the lad replies. "Are you sure?" the politician pressed, but the boy declined payment. 'Well, is there anything I can do for you? What do you want to be when you grow up?' The boy responded, "I want to be a doctor." The Member of Parliament offered to help the young Scot go to university, and sure enough, he followed through on his pledge. More than a half-century later, Winston Churchill lay dangerously ill with pneumonia, stricken while attending a wartime conference in Morocco. A new 'wonder drug' was administered to him, a drug called penicillin that Sir Alexander Fleming had discovered. You've guessed it: Fleming was the young Scottish lad who came to the aid of the Member of Parliament. The member of Parliament was none other than Randolph Churchill, Winston Churchill's father.

While historians point out that this story may not be historically verified in its details, and there's no direct evidence of such an exchange between Fleming and the Churchill family, its message continues to inspire: Yes, what goes around comes around.

Please note that **Asset Fathers** are not immune from the challenges of fatherhood, which are many, especially in the 21st century; they have only developed coping strategies to excel despite them.

Practically every father encounters significant challenges in fulfilling their roles. Societal expectations, economic pressures, and the demands of work-life balance stare everyone in the face, hindering their ability to be present and engaged.

Below are some challenges of Fatherhood in the 21st Century:

1. **Work-Life Balance**: Many fathers struggle to balance their professional responsibilities with family time. The demands of modern jobs where many offices are open 24 hours based on globalization often lead to long hours and increased stress, making it difficult for parents to be present for their children.

   Possible solution: Ensure your family is carried along with your work schedule; this gives them hope to look forward to their time with you. Also, attach the same importance you give your profession to your family. So, set clear boundaries for the two so that one does not cannibalize the other.

   There is a poem that says:

Work while you work
Play while you play.
One thing each time,
That is the way.
All that you do,
Do with your might.
Things done by halves
Are never done right.

2. **Changing Gender Roles**: As traditional gender roles evolve, fathers are increasingly expected to be more involved in childcare and household duties. This shift can create pressure as they navigate expectations both at home and in the workplace.

    Possible Solution: Change is the only constant thing in life, and anyone who refuses a peaceful change will be forcefully changed. Acknowledge this truth and make necessary adjustments so that whichever side of the divide you find yourself, you will adapt. Please discuss your willingness to adapt to your family's needs and request their patience as you make the necessary changes. Remember, adaptability is the easy path to survival.

3. **Health Awareness**: Fathers often focus on their families' health but may neglect their own. Encouraging self-care and maintaining physical health can be difficult amidst other responsibilities. Overall, the landscape of fatherhood is evolving, presenting both new challenges and opportunities for fathers to engage meaningfully with their children and families.

The traditional concept of men's invincibility has sent many men into untimely graves. We try to "man" every challenge and keep bottling things up until it gets out of hand. There is a growing recognition of mental health issues, but many fathers may feel societal pressure to appear strong and invincible. This can lead to challenges in seeking help for stress, anxiety, or depression.

Possible Solution: Do not be deceived; the best of men are still men at their best.

Humble yourself to seek help where there is a need for it so that the situation does not humble you more, irreparably.

There is nothing wrong with a man being sick; however, there is everything wrong with living in denial. Acknowledge your need for medical help and seek one when needed.

Note: The best form of healthcare is preventive medicine, which includes eating right, sleeping right, exercising right, and resting right. Do not wait until things break down before you do damage control; regular medical checks are not out of place.

Self-care is not selfishness; it is only being a good steward of yourself so you can be alive and well to serve the best of yourself to others.

Take your health seriously, and more importantly, your mental health. Consult the experts when needed. Connect with a faith-based group (The Living Church) where you can detoxify and recharge your mind with the most potent instrument–The Bible (The Word of God).

4. **Economic Pressure**: Economic instability, rising living costs, and job insecurity can stress fathers significantly. This financial burden can impact their ability to provide for their families, leading to feelings of inadequacy. Nothing demoralizes a man like his inability to cater for those he loves.

Possible Solution: Having worked hard but constantly noticing that your "take home" (income) cannot take you home, try the following:

a. Call for an emergency council meeting in your home and fully disclose your financial situation. That sounds demeaning, but it is beneficial. It helps everyone see the potential danger and the need for an urgent change. It will also ease the financial burden on your heart and most likely earn their sympathy.

b. Draw up a budget that your income can support. There could be a need to cut off some financial fats and some excess luggage, but that is fine.

c. Adhere strictly to the budget as you try to improve your earning capacity. When your children ask why they cannot enjoy some fancy toys like others, encourage them it is not accommodable now, but you will definitely get there later. Jim Rohn says, "When your outflow exceeds your inflow, your upkeep becomes your downfall."

d. Encourage giving to God and the people. Giving is like planting; it is an opportunity to put a seed down for a future harvest.

e. Encourage savings and investment. Let your family know this is the pathway to a better financial future.

f. Avoid debts, especially consumer debts, as much as possible because that is the surest pathway to a lifetime of modern slavery. Whatever you cannot accommodate within your income means you cannot afford it yet, except it will produce returns that will far outweigh its cost. Godliness with contentment is great gain.

Please note that I am not a financial expert; I am just talking from my experience. You may want to consult a financial consultant for your peculiar situation.

5. **Fathers facing divorce or separation often encounter unique co-parenting difficulties**: Navigating relationships with ex-partners while ensuring the well-being of their children can be complicated and emotionally taxing.

Possible Solution:

a. Ask God for wisdom to handle the complication.

b. Never talk down on your ex-partner, no matter what.

c. Own up to your children; you and your partner have disappointed them, but you will do your best to manage the situation.

d. Never shy away from disciplining your children when needed. Do not try to play the "good dad syndrome" and look away from their misbehavior.

e. Be involved in your children's lives as much as possible. Never see them as an avenue to get back at your ex-partner.

6. **Access to Resources: The absence of readily available parenting resources and support networks makes it hard for many fathers to seek advice or share experiences.**

    Possible Solution: The Bible, especially the book of Proverbs, is an invaluable resource from which you can garner wisdom on parenting. You could connect with other men in your church or start a men's group to create a forum for open dialogue for men in your church. Technology has made information easily accessible to all. To avoid misinformation, carefully review online information.

7. **Cultural Expectations**: Fathers may face cultural or societal expectations that dictate how they should parent, leading to stress when their parenting style differs from these norms.

    Possible Solution: Your faith should form the foundation for everything you do. My faith, Christianity, teaches me that children might have come through me, but are not from me; they are God's own. Therefore, I will parent according to God's will, not cultural norms. The Bible, with its insights into God's mind, guides me on every issue, especially parenting.

8. **Technology and Parenting**: The rise of technology presents both challenges and opportunities for parenting. Fathers must navigate screen time, social media, and digital safety issues while integrating technology into their parenting approach.

Possible Solution: Fathers can leverage technology for better parenting by continually upgrading their tech skills and embracing growth.

It takes learning and growing to keep winning and gaining the respect of others.

TIME FOR REflECTION

1. What do you find most captivating in this chapter?

\
\
\
\
\

2. Based on the new insights gained, what commitment(s) will you make?

\
\
\
\
\

3. What are your action steps to implement your commitment(s)?

\
\
\
\
\

CHAPTER 4

Notable Traits of a Great Father

> *"My father didn't tell me how to live. He lived, and let me watch him do it."*
> **- Clarence Budington Kelland.**

It's crucial to understand from the start that this list of great father traits isn't exhaustive.

Also, it is worth noting that these are not racially, socially, or geographically biased; some or all are universally conspicuous in the life of a great but not perfect father.

There is no better father to use as a standard of a great father than the Father of all fathers, Abba, The Source of all things: God. Jesus made us see that God is not just our creator, but also our heavenly Father.

God's fatherhood has been acclaimed to be the best ever known, so the best way to capture the notable traits of a responsible father is to consider the notable traits of our heavenly Father.

1. <u>**Love:**</u> The most notable trait of God is love, and every responsible father must have it too.

   "Beloved, let us love one another, for love is of God; and everyone who loves is born of God and knows God. He who does not love does not know God, **for God is love." 1 John 4:7-8 (NKJV)**

   Jesus Christ, the Son of God, exemplified the trait of His Father; this is to validate the truth that, like father, like son.

   If God is truly your Father too, you must have this all-important trait in you to be a responsible father, representing the heavenly Father in your family.

   Giving is the proof of love, "for God so love the world that He gave"–**John 3:16.** It is possible to give without love, but it is impossible to have this notable trait called love without giving.

   Love can be classified into two groups.

- **Compassionate love**–This dimension of love shows kindness, empathy, and sacrifice.

   Nature makes a father to be kind and compassionate, as the bible says below:

   "As a father is kind to his children, so the LORD is kind to those who honor him" - **Psalm 103:13 GNT.**

- Tough love–This is the dimension of love that corrects and disciplines.

   "And have you forgotten God's encouraging words to you, his child? He said, 'My son, don't be angry when the Lord punishes you. Don't be discouraged when he has to show you where you are wrong. For when he

punishes you, it proves that he loves you. When he whips you, it proves you are really his child." Let God train you, for he is doing what any loving father does for his children—whoever heard of a son who was never corrected?" **- Hebrews 12:5-7 TLB.**

A responsible father doesn't just tell you that he loves you; he shows it by giving compassion and discipline. Responsible fathers are profoundly tender and passionately affectionate to God, the family, and others.
*"Besides all these, you must have love. This joins everything together as it should be"***–Colossians 3:14 (WE).**

Love is one trait that captures every other trait; no wonder Jesus Christ says, "Love is the fulfillment of the law"–**Romans 13:10 NKJV.** All the fame and success in the world couldn't replace the unexpressed love of a father. Parental love isn't something that a child should have to wonder about or search for. It shouldn't be given only during good times, when things are easy, or when they succeed or make you proud. You need to always express your love verbally because love is a trait that shows you are a responsible father. You are here to serve your child, whatever that may look like: cooking meals, tying shoelaces, taking them to the doctor, and keeping them safe. Your child doesn't have to earn these things. They didn't ask to be here, and you have no place denying them love, even for a second. Remind them of their inherent worth, regardless of their circumstances or actions. Refrain from asking them to make you proud. It implies that they owe you something, or that it's possible to disappoint you. Your love must go beyond being a reward but a requirement you give to show your fatherhood; at least none of us earned the selfless love of God, our heavenly father.

"But God showed His great love for us by sending Christ to die for us while we were still sinners" - **Romans 5:8 TLB.**

Check out your love grade with your children by pulling this trick; when next you see your child playing, call him and say, hey, there's something I need to tell you. Pause for a bit and see his reaction. What is he expecting? Now, tell your child you love him. Is he surprised or confused? If something so simple and true catches him off guard, that speaks volumes about you and the expectations you've built. Maybe that's an area of yourself you may need to work on. Because no father gets to the end of his life and wishes he had said less, "I love you." Your child may forget your laws, but he will never forget your love.

2. **Leadership**: One of the natural traits of a responsible father is leadership. The mandate of Dominion given to man validates his leadership trait.

Leading by Example:
Setting a positive example for your children. Responsible fathers have the noblest call to cultivate their leadership traits and become great leaders, not just good ones. Good leaders are eager to find a way, but great leaders are willing to make a way. Good leaders are concerned about income, but great leaders are worried about the impact.

Good leaders are goal-driven, but great leaders are God-driven.

Good leaders develop products, but great leaders develop people.

Good leaders could labor to be famous, but great leaders labor to be faithful.

Good leaders are concerned with being admired, but great leaders are concerned with advancement.

Good leaders are concerned about the present, but great leaders are concerned about the future–legacy.

Good leaders are role models at work alone, but great leaders are role models in life at large.

John C. Maxwell says, "A leader is the one who knows the way, goes the way, and shows the way."

Good leadership could be defined as being a good example.

A responsible father does not operate by the old slogan 'do as I say, not as I do'.

Jesus Christ confirmed that our heavenly father, our standard of fatherhood, lives by example.

"Then Jesus answered and said to them, "Most assuredly, I say to you, the Son can do nothing of Himself, but what He sees the Father do; for whatever He does, the Son also does in like manner" - **John 5:19 NKJV.**

God never requested holiness from man when He is not; He says, "Be holy for I am holy"–**Leviticus 19:2 NKJV.**

God never asked us to love until He showed us love; "As I have loved you, that you also love one another" - **John 13:34 NKJV & 1 John 4:19 NKJV.**

God, the Father's modeling lifestyle, is also revealed in **2 Corinthians 1:4 NKJV** when He says, *"Comfort others with the same comfort you have been comforted."* He comforts us first before asking us to comfort others.

- **The power of your actions.**

  Never forget that actions speak louder than words. Please don't confuse your children as you teach them; never allow your actions to contradict your intentions or words.
  I need to admit something to you now. I am not proud of this at all, as I am very guilty of the same sin I condemned others for; nevertheless, I will share it all because I know it could help some fathers.

  This is my true-life story in conjunction with my sons in the car, who were both 6 years old.

  I teach my children to be law-abiding everywhere they go, and they make efforts (as much as I know) to keep to that.

  When I drive, I usually max out the speed limit on the road, and sometimes, when I'm running late for a meeting, I go above the speed limit (I am not proud of that at all).

  One day, I was driving, and I heard my sons conversing:

Son 1 - When I start driving, I would love to speed; I hate vehicles moving slowly.

Son 2: You cannot do that because every road has a speed limit.

Son 1: That does not matter; I will still speed because I enjoy vehicles moving really fast.

Son 2: If you do that, you will not be a law-abiding citizen, as Daddy has taught us.

And the Police can pull you over, which may mess up your record with the government.

Son 1: That's not true. Are you saying Daddy is not a law-abiding citizen? He is constantly speeding. He never keeps to the speed limit on the road.

Son 2: I don't know; maybe Daddy can say something about that.

Wow, I was thoroughly embarrassed as my son invited me to join the conversation. For once, I was ashamed of myself. I softly responded like a weather-beaten chicken: I am sorry, I was wrong.

Let's always keep to the speed limit.

From that day, I changed my way. I am more conscious of obeying the road signs and instructions because it is not about me now, but the next generation.

If they can't trust me to do what I say when I am behind the wheel, they might begin to doubt every other word of instruction and counsel I give too.

Fathers, let's be careful; what we are doing might be so loud that our children can't hear what we're saying.

Your child is like your mirror; he only reflects what you placed before him.

Dorothy Lew Nolte, in her poem, says the following:

If a child lives with criticism, He learns to condemn.

If a child lives with hostility, He learns to fight.

If a child lives with ridicule, He learns to be shy.

If a child lives with shame, He learns to feel guilty.

If a child lives with tolerance, He learns to be patient.

If a child lives with encouragement, He learns confidence.

If a child lives with praise, He learns to appreciate people.

If a child lives with fairness, He learns justice.

If a child lives with security, He learns to have faith.

If a child lives with approval, He learns to like himself.

If a child lives with acceptance and friendship, He learns to find love in the world.

Fathers must acknowledge that our children's urgent and most important need is not a moderator but a model.

It is mandatory to show them what it means to do the right thing, not just to tell them.

Imagine you're driving your car. Your child is sitting in the back seat, watching, just like mine. You're hurrying to reach your destination, so you drive too fast and get pulled over.

To salvage the already stressed family finances, you try to lie that you were not speeding but failed to talk your way out of the ticket. After the Police Officer leaves, you mutter your annoyance and frustration under your breath. To you, that might be just another stressful day. But your child was observing you the whole time. What lessons did they learn or unlearn? You can't stress the importance of following rules and speeding when convenient.

What's the value of honesty if you lie to the Police Officer to avoid a fine? We often preach love and respect and then say bad things behind other people's back. It's not just isolated moments like this that count, we need to be conscious of the fact that our children are always watching us from the back seat. They're following us. And when we go off the path, so do they.

When next your child does something you disapprove of, ask them this: have you ever seen me do that? Maybe you've been unconsciously or accidentally modeling unhealthy behavior like I did.

But now we have a valuable learning opportunity to be better. Our children are always watching. We must be careful and intentional in modeling the right thing before them.

3. **Living a life of integrity and purpose.**

    Integrity: This trait is notable in God, and every responsible father must have it. God is dependable; His integrity is second to none.

    "God is not a man, that He should lie, nor a son of man, that He should repent. Has He said, and will He not do? Or has He spoken, and will He not make it good?" **- Numbers 23:19 NKJV.**

    "So, it is impossible for God to lie, for we know that his promise and his vow will never change! And now we have run into his heart to hide ourselves in his faithfulness. This is where we find his strength and comfort, for he empowers us to seize what has already been established ahead of time—an unshakable hope!" **- Hebrews 6:18 TPT.**

Every responsible father has a notable trait of adhering strictly to moral and ethical principles. They have sound moral character–they mean what they say and say what they mean.

> *"For we are taking pains to do what is right, not only in the eyes of the Lord but also in the eyes of man,"*
> *- 2 Corinthians 8:21 NIV.*

• **Responsibility**: Fatherhood is not about title, but responsibility. A well-groomed beard, broad chest with a six-pack, six-foot height, or six-figure income never defines responsible fathers.

Responsibility is all about keeping and being accountable for what is committed to your care.

Adam, the first father, lost his garden of comfort–Eden because he couldn't give a proper account of the activities within his household.

God, the epitome of responsible fatherhood, displays this trait as He is responsible for keeping all His creations. The following bible passages authenticate God as being responsible:

> *"Look at the birds of the air, for they neither sow nor reap nor gather into barns; yet your heavenly Father feeds them. Are you not of more value than they?"*
> *- Matthew 6:26 NKJV.*
>
> *"For I will do whatever you ask me to do when you ask me in my name. And that is how the Son will show what the Father is really like and bring glory to him"*
> *- John 14:13 TPT.*
>
> *"I promise that I will never leave you helpless or abandon you as orphans - I will come back to you"*
> *- John 14:18 TPT.*

Attempting to take responsibility for others without taking personal responsibility will be deceptive. Fathers must take personal responsibility for their joy, peace, and self-motivation.

Every responsible father owns the key to his own ignition switch.

- **<u>Nobility</u>**: A responsible father has the trait of acting honorably. Responsible fathers are distinguished people who have the trait of royalty, and they always stand out for good.

> *"But we are a chosen generation, a royal priesthood, a holy nation, His own special people, that we may proclaim the praises of Him who called us out of darkness into His marvelous light"*
> *- 1 Peter 2:9 NKJV.*

Responsible fathers honor people, including their children.

> *"Jesus answered, "If I honor Myself, My honor is nothing. It is My Father who honors Me, of whom you say that He is your God"*
> *- John 8:54 NKJV.*

Fathers should also learn from Jesus's teaching that it is not enough to demand obedience and compliance from our children. Fathers should note that it is very noble to honor their children.

4. **<u>Courage</u>**–Responsible fathers have the quality of mind and spirit to face and overcome whatever challenges come their way.

They are not rascals running a hopeless race; they are of the tribe of the Lion of Judah enlisted in a winning race.

> *"For God has not given us a spirit of fear, but of power and of love and of a sound mind"*
> *- 2 Timothy 1:7 NKJV.*

Remember, we are all born fearless; along the path of our growth, the world around us teaches us their fears.

A child will attempt to hold fire until the world around him inputs the fear of fire into him. The same goes for every other thing we are afraid of today; someone, someday, somewhere, must have taught us that we are unable, or it is impossible.

If we learn our fears, we can, therefore, unlearn them. Courageous fathers must impact this trait on their descendants by encouraging them to be audacious, daring, and bold.

> *"There's no shame in fear, my father told me; what matters is how we face it."*
> **- George R.R. Martin, A Clash of Kings.**

TIME FOR REflECTION

1. What do you find most captivating in this chapter?

____

____

____

____

2. Based on the new insights gained, what commitment(s) will you make?

____

____

____

____

3. What are your action steps to implement your commitment(s)?

____

____

____

____

CHAPTER 5

Roles of Fatherhood

> *"I cannot think of any need in childhood as strong as the need for a father's protection."*
> *- Sigmund Freud.*

It's quite demanding to be a father, not to mention in the 21st century. Fathers are under more pressure in this dispensation than ever in human history.

A great father embodies many responsibilities that extend far beyond mere provision. His role is multifaceted, encompassing emotional support, guidance, and being a role model.

Firstly, emotional nurturing is one of the most vital responsibilities of a great father. A father should create a safe and supportive environment where children feel secure in expressing their thoughts and emotions. This involves active listening, showing empathy, and being available to discuss any concerns or joys in their lives. When children know they can rely on their father for emotional support, it fosters a strong bond and builds their self-esteem. Moreover, a father should guide his children in moral and ethical decisions, teaching them responsibility, respect, and integrity.

God holds fathers responsible for whatever happens in their homes because they are called to lead their families.

As a father, it is dangerous to delegate the role of decision-making to any other person. It is risky to make a collective decision; you are expected to consider your wife's and children's opinions. You may even seek counsel from relatives, friends, colleagues, mentors, and spiritual leaders. However, never forget that the buck stops at your desk because you will ultimately be responsible for whatever happens in your family.

The consequences of your choice cannot be prayed away, so make your choice with a clear mind and the help of the Holy Spirit.

Fathers are like a building's foundation; it's not that all other parts of the building are unnecessary, but the stability of all different parts of the building depends on the foundation (fathers).

When God came to the Garden of Eden, He didn't call for Eve; He called for Adam because He is meant to be responsible for his household.

I understand that you are not responsible for your past and how your ancestors raised you. However, the good news is that if you arise today as a father, you can positively influence your descendants.

Family is God's perfect solution to global unrest and institutional failures, not politics, policies, or programs.

If you walk away from raising your family, never complain about societal decadence because you contributed to it by your negligence.

If we can fix our families, then we can fix the world because that's where it all begins.

Family should be where you are built up, not torn down. If you do it right, it should be a place of empowerment and stability.

God intends that the blessing (inheritance) He gives to every family should be transgenerational. For this to happen, every father must communicate God's blessing and inheritance to the subsequent generations.

> *"Now therefore, in the sight of all Israel, the assembly of the LORD, and in the hearing of our God, be careful to seek out all the commandments of the LORD your God, that you may possess this good land, and leave it as an inheritance for your children after you forever."*
> **- 1 Chronicles 28:8 NKJV.**

The world has erroneously limited the definition of fatherhood to making babies, so it's easy to be a father, but it's hard to be one indeed.

Any man can make babies, but it takes a real man with a spine to be a father. Fatherhood is all about pouring yourself into others.

God expects fathers to fulfill many responsibilities to raise a godly family. Still, I will attempt to summarize them alongside the biblical meaning of who a father is.

The root word for father in Hebrew is abba, which refers to source or sustainer. Fathers are called to be the source of their family: source of identity, vision, protection, provision, etc.

Below are some responsibilities of a father, even though it is not exhaustive:

1. **Fathers must be a Source of Spirituality**–If the God of the fathers will be the God of their succeeding generations, there must be transference. Fathers are primarily responsible for connecting their children to the Living God, the Source of all things.

This cannot be casually done; it takes a lot of intentionality, as there is a devil who is hell-bent on cutting the flow of God's blessing from one generation to another. It takes more than taking the family to church on Sundays; you must be careful to bring the church to your home daily.

This issue of spiritual guidance is so important to God that He instructed the Israelites thus:

> *"Listen, O Israel! The LORD is our God, the LORD alone. And you must love the LORD your God with all your heart, all your soul, and all your strength. And you must commit yourselves wholeheartedly to these commands that I am giving you today. Repeat them again and again to your children. Talk about them when you are at home and when you are on the road, when you are going to bed, and when you are getting up. Tie them to your hands and wear them on your forehead as reminders. Write them on the doorposts of your house and on your gates,"*
> **- Deuteronomy 6:4-9 NLT.**

Every father must ensure they have a family prayer altar in their home. Keep the family prayer altar alive no matter what you do outside your home.

- **Never forget that it's a successful failure who succeeds in everything but fails in raising a godly family.**

The devil is not afraid of the degrees and pedigrees of your children; he can even use all those for his advantage once he rules their spirits. The devil is only intimidated by your descendants wired with the Word and strengthened by the Spirit of God; such is the seed of a woman that will crush the head of the serpent anywhere.

- **Any generation you give gold without God will eventually turn the gold to God.**

2. **Fathers must be a Source of Provision:** Fathers are called to model the true God to their families, and one of God's key attributes is that He provides for all His creations. So, any father who fails to provide is failing in his duty.

Provision is a fundamental responsibility. While financial support is a significant aspect of this, true provision goes beyond material needs. A great father ensures that his children have access to healthcare, education, and opportunities for personal growth.

> *"Anyone who does not provide for their relatives, and especially for their own household, has denied the faith and is worse than an unbeliever"*
> *- 1 Timothy 5:8 NIV.*

The proof of fatherhood is in your benevolence - If you, being evil, know how to give good gifts to your sons, how much more will your Heavenly Father give - **Luke 11:13.**

As a father, you are expected to provide much more than resources; you are to provide love, attention, and quality time to nurture and enrich.

Your family doesn't just need your presents (gifts); they need your presence even more (be there for them).

You cannot train a child online. AI (Artificial Intelligence) is insufficient; can anything replace your presence?

It is essential that fathers focus their prayers on their finances because Satan will always want to stop them from being providers so that they can fail on their first assignment of being providers.

3. **Fathers must be a Source of Identity** - The genesis of the first man's (Adam) downfall was an identity crisis. The devil tricked him into believing that he was not who God said he was. When the devil also came to Jesus Christ, the last Adam, he employed the same strategy. He wanted to trick him into believing that He was not who God said He was.

Identity crises are widespread, with young teenagers being the most vulnerable age group. A 2015 study revealed that 37% of teenagers had trouble discovering their identity, and 95% felt inferior.

The excerpt below was from the article, Social Media, Suicidal Thoughts and an Identity Crisis Among Young Adults, written by Cara McNulty and Taft Parsons III, MD.

"The journey into and through young adulthood is a pivotal and complex period of identity formation. Although this can be a positive time of self-discovery, it often can be marked by uncertainty or self-doubt as well, compounding with academic, financial, and relationship stressors to create feelings of desperation and hopelessness. And when this generation watches their peers have an 'easier' time online, with celebratory photos of life events and nights out, it can feel like they are not transitioning into adulthood the 'right way'.

This exemplifies how using social media is a double-edged sword. It provides a platform for self-expression while simultaneously fueling unrealistic standards and a constant desire for validation. Incessant comparisons to peers, celebrities, and influencers can intensify a young person's internal struggle to align their personal identity with societal standards and ideals.

This excerpt alluded to the fact that social media has worsened the identity crisis in the 21ˢᵗ Century, as envy and bullying are easily fabricated in cyberspace.

Identity is simply answering the question of, "Who am I?

So, fathers are to provide identity for their children; leaving such a destiny-defining responsibility to others is dangerous. It is so safe and appropriate that the branch takes its identity from the tree.

Knowing who you are and whose you are frees you from the opinion of others. People will always want you to rise and fall according to their views of you, but that is the origin of identity crises.

So, what is an identity crisis?

An identity crisis is a period of confusion and doubt surrounding one's sense of self. It often occurs during transition or when someone is forced to confront aspects of their life that conflict with the roles they have taken on.

Identity is a complex interplay of various factors, including:

- **Personal identity**: As a father, what are the characteristics, such as personality, values, beliefs, and goals peculiar to you and your family?

- **Social identity**: How do you define yourself and your family in relation to your tribe, nationality, or religion?

- **Cultural identity**: As a father, what beliefs, customs, and traditions do you identify with? Are they ungodly or godly, limiting or unrestrictive, enslaving or empowering?

- **Gender identity**: Your sexual orientation. According to God's word, which is the eternal truth and final authority over all creation, you are either a male or a female. This does not change throughout your life; anything different from this simple truth is evil and immoral.

Identity is a lifelong process that experiences, relationships, and societal influences could shape. It's fluid and can change over time, but the unchanging word of God (The Bible) must be used as a benchmark for any identity you adopt.

As a father, your identity must be rooted in your convictions, which must be clearly communicated to the next generation so that they do not blend in with a world of people that is bankrupt of identity.

Let your children know that **God never created them to blend in but to stand out.** They do not need to apologize to the world for their difference but see it as a uniqueness that will compel the attention of their world.

Your convictions are clearly seen in the values you live by. A father must set values to guide the family - Joshua was unapologetic about it when he says:

> *"But if you refuse to serve the LORD, then choose today whom you will serve. Would you prefer the gods your ancestors served beyond the Euphrates? Or will it be the gods of the Amorites in whose land you now live? But as for me and my family, we will serve the LORD"*

> *- Joshua 24:15 NLT.*

Values act as boundaries that help guide and guard your life. They help you stand for something so you do not fall for everything.

- **Remember, life does not value anyone who lacks values. Please don't sell your children cheaply; give them godly values to live by.**

4. **Fathers must be a Source of vision -** The father is the head of the family, and as we all know, the head houses the eyes we use to see.

As a father, you are expected to see the following for the family:

- **Danger**: As a father playing your roles well, you are expected to foresee danger and devise a strategy to save your family from it. This danger could be physical, economic, spiritual, or emotional.

For example, Joseph played the role of a father for Baby Jesus when He was on earth, and Joseph was the one who saw through his dream that the murderer called Herod was coming for the life of Baby Jesus. He promptly relocated the family to Egypt from Judah to ensure his family's safety.

Your spiritual sensitivity should be red alert to discern your children's associations that are dangerous to their destiny so that you can wisely pull them out of it.

To safeguard your children's future, you need to be sensitive enough to identify the danger in the violent and immoral materials they watch and intervene before it affects them.

You should also identify those habits and quirks that could act as viruses and corrupt your children's glorious destiny; you must nip such in the bud before it becomes a monster that will be difficult to tame.

Opportunities: As a father, you are not just expected to spot dangers but also opportunities that will give an advantage to your family.

How can each generation surpass its predecessor?

It is simply by one generation handing down opportunities and advantages to the next.

Any unconquered territory becomes a slippery ground for the next generation.

One of the most significant opportunities, low-hanging fruit, and a complete game changer you must spot and give to your family is the salvation of their souls.

Remember how far you have wandered and how many years you have wasted in ignorance, groping in the dark, looking for help where there was none until the opportunity of being saved by Jesus Christ was extended to you.

Your family members must not suffer this or waste their years searching for what is not lost. Give them the opportunity to accept Jesus Christ as their personal Lord and Savior early. Create the opportunity for them to be saved at every slightest chance in a non-threatening manner, and I believe they will embrace Jesus Christ and be grateful that you did.

The Bible says to talk about God (and His salvation offer) at the dining table, when on a trip, at bedtime, at the gym, etc.–**Deuteronomy 6:6-9.**

You can create opportunities for your family by repositioning them in systems and environments that leverage their greatest skills, even if they haven't recognized them.

Consider moving them to a society or environment that could give them access to better education, jobs, and social networks, helping them reach their full potential.

More so, Helen Keller says, "The only thing worse than being blind is having sight without vision."

Vision is more than the perception of sight; vision is the picture of the future producing passion.

Every father should have a vision statement that paints the picture of his family's future, and that picture should be compelling enough to produce passion in every family member.

> *"Write the vision down and make it plain on tablets, that he may run who reads it"*
> *- Habakkuk 2:2.*

There cannot be runners without a vision; give your children something to run with until they can discover their own, or else they will run with other people's vision that could derail or be detrimental to their destiny.

It does not have to be complicated; the simpler it is, the more potent it will be. It could be as simple as being a godly pacesetter in everything you do.

Please note that your vision is not meant to be designed; it is to be discovered. God is your creator, and He had a purpose in mind for creating you. Go to Him to ask for your vision, and He will reveal it to you.

5. **Fathers must be a Source of Protection**–Being protective is one of a father's most profound responsibilities. Children often blossom and excel in a safe environment. A great father does not just protect his family from the obvious dangers but also from the undisclosed ones that sneak in through the airwaves (social media and the internet) and the enemies within (laziness, indiscipline, selfishness, and self-centeredness) that could act as a virus and corrupt a great destiny unsuspectingly. To protect is to keep safe, to stop any danger from gaining entrance into your family - **John 17:12.**

These are some of the things you must protect as a father:

- Protect the lives of your household members.

- Protect your family's values against those who don't have theirs. *(Discipline must be a process of protecting values and destiny).*

- Protect your family's inheritance and traditions.

- Protect your family's identity

- Protect the destinies of your children from the destiny destroyers.

> *"I cannot think of any need in children as strong as the need for a father's protection."*
> *- **Sigmund Freud.***

Additionally, a father must protect his children physically and emotionally from harm. This includes creating a safe home environment and being vigilant about the influences in their lives.

Tips for Interacting with Children Who Need Extra Grace

I am cautious not to label any child as difficult or stubborn, as several factors could be responsible for their unconventionality beyond their control. So, we must cease name-calling, as that has never helped, and it will never help.

Below are some tips that could help in reconciling or rebuilding the broken relationship with your children:

1. Children are God's own, not yours. They may have come through you, but they are not from you. Take them back to their owner in prayers instead of nagging and complaining. Pray more for them and talk less, especially when the child is an adult.

2. Stop querying and questioning; start discussing sincerely with the intention of seeing through their lens, not judging.

3. Avoid asking, "Why aren't you interested in your schoolwork?" Instead, try an open-ended question: "I perceive there are other areas of interest you have. I'd love to hear what interests you. Would you love to share it with me?".

The emotionally intelligent response is to be curious about where your child's motivation and abilities intersect so you can guide them appropriately.

4. If you're locked in a disagreement with a seemingly difficult child, instead of asking them why they don't listen, consider asking, "Have I listened to you?"

Children's brains are wired for autonomy and a need to explore the world based on their own identity, not your beliefs about who they should be.

So, avoid striving for compliance from your children, but for connection. They need to know you are willing to hear the truth of their experience.

5. Avoid comparison; two children are never the same. Comparison is counterproductive. Each child possesses a unique gift; help them discover and develop it.

6. Completely avoid public embarrassment; this will do far more damage to them than you might think. Their self-esteem and self-worth might be affected in the process.

7. Be a role model yourself. You are the mirror placed before your children; they will most effortlessly reflect what you put before them. You may need to work on yourself deliberately in the area where you expect a change in your children. If your children dislikes doing homework, when last did they see you with a book, too? Or are you always on the phone chatting but insisting that they stay on their book; it may not work.

In conclusion, the responsibilities of a great father are vast and impactful. Through emotional nurturing, guidance, education, provision, and protection, a father plays a crucial role in shaping the lives of his children. The influence of a great father extends beyond the immediate family, impacting society as a whole by raising well-rounded, responsible individuals who contribute positively to their communities. Ultimately, the legacy of a great father is not merely in the financial stability he provides but in the love, support, and values he instills in his children.

TIME FOR REflECTION

1. What do you find most captivating in this chapter?

2. Based on the new insights gained, what commitment(s) will you make?

3. What are your action steps to implement your commitment(s)?

CHAPTER 6

Legacy-Minded Fatherhood

> *"A father's love still travels on after he's gone. A treasure hidden in the hearts of his children."*
> **- John Mark Green.**

Fathers play a pivotal role in shaping not only their children's lives but also the broader legacy that their families will carry into the future. As such, it is essential for fathers to adopt a legacy-minded approach. This mindset involves being intentional about the values, traditions, and teachings they impart, ensuring that their influence extends beyond their lifetime.

Firstly, a legacy-minded father understands the importance of values. By instilling core principles such as honesty, integrity, and respect, fathers can help their children navigate the complexities of life. These values serve as a foundation, guiding children in their decisions and interactions with others. When fathers model these behaviors, they create an environment where children can learn the significance of character, ultimately impacting their relationships and contributions to society.

Secondly, traditions play a crucial role in family dynamics. Legacy-minded fathers actively create and maintain family traditions, whether through holidays, rituals, or shared activities. These traditions foster a sense of belonging and continuity, helping children feel connected to their heritage. When children participate in family traditions, they develop a deeper understanding of their identity and the values that define their family. This connection encourages them to carry these traditions forward, perpetuating a sense of legacy through generations. Moreover, education is a vital aspect of a father's legacy. A legacy-minded father prioritizes his children's education, not only academically but also emotionally and socially.

Training your children today for their reigning tomorrow

The Bible passages below validate that God is a teacher, and He wants the fathers representing Him in the family to be teachers to their families, too.

> *"And they have turned to Me the back, not the face; though I taught them, rising up early and teaching them, yet they have not listened to receive instruction."*
> *- Jeremiah 32:33 NKJV*
>
> *"All your children shall be taught by the LORD, and great shall be the peace of your children."*
> *- Isaiah 54:13 NKJV*

Children do not lack the capacity to learn; they only lack teachers who will accept responsibility for sowing the seeds of knowledge and avert the invasion of weeds in the rich soil of their curious minds.

> *"You shall teach them diligently to your children and shall talk of them when you sit in your house, when you walk by the way, when you lie down, and when you rise up."*
> **- Deuteronomy 6:7 NKJV**

Dr. Mike Murdock says, "The greatest investment a parent can make is the one they make in their children."

Fathers must arise and teach the next generation to avoid repeating the blunders of the past and missing out on the opportunities of the future.

The teaching should include the following and even more:

- **Teach them about your God**–Teach them how to call on God (pray) and how to hear God speak to them through His word and His Holy Spirit.

- **Financial Management**–Exposing the children to the truth that resources gravitate towards value, not wishes, is critical. As soon as they can identify money, teach them how to make, save, invest, and spend one.
  Let them know that if their outflow exceeds their inflow, their upkeep may become their downfall, so they must budget.

- **To delay gratification**–Teach your children to learn to delay gratification. Every time your children show boundless desperation for their desires, they create an avenue for people to take undue advantage of them. So, teach your children to mask their hunger.

> *"Hungry people make poor shoppers."*
> **- Robin Norwood.**

- **The law of sowing and reaping—**teach your children that wrong actions attract punishment, and right actions come with rewards.

  Let your children know that their present actions will inevitably shape their future consequences.

  The worst form of deception is self-deception, and the height of self-deception is to keep sowing bad seeds while praying for the harvest not to come. God's justice system will always make us reap what we sow, even if not where we sow.

  o   Our maturity can be seen in our ability to sow seeds without complaining and reap a harvest without apologizing to the envious.

> *"If the past cannot teach the present, and the father cannot teach the son, then history need not have bothered to go on, and the world has wasted a great deal of time."*
> **- Russell Hoban.**

Fathers must equip their children with the necessary tools to succeed in an ever-changing world by encouraging curiosity, critical thinking, and resilience. This investment in their training ensures that children are prepared to take on challenges and make meaningful contributions to society, reinforcing the father's legacy through their accomplishments and character.

These are some ways to teach your children to grow and become godly and responsible adults:

1. **Teach your family through what they see you do - Proverbs 23:26.**

> *"My son, give me your heart and let your eyes observe my ways"*
> *- Proverbs 23:26.*

Your conduct today as a father becomes the standard that your children will live by tomorrow.

- If the standard upheld by your children is low, it's a sign that your conduct as a father is poor.

2. **Teach your family through what you permit.**

> *I will set nothing wicked before my eyes; I hate the work of those who fall away; It shall not cling to me."*
> *- Psalm 101:3 NKJV.*

> *"Let love be without hypocrisy. Abhor what is evil. Cling to what is good".*
> *- Romans 12:9 NKJV.*

If you permit evil around you, no matter how much you love righteousness, you cannot be a successful father.

> *"You love righteousness and hate wickedness; Therefore God, Your God, has anointed You With the oil of gladness more than Your companions."*
> *- Psalm 45:7 NKJV.*

Don't permit the wrong influencers around you.

> *"Do not be deceived: "Evil company corrupts good habits."*
> *- 1 Corinthians 15:33 NKJV*

- **Whatever you don't want, you don't watch.**

3. **Teach your family through what you seek or pursue–**

> *"O God, You are my God; Early will I seek You; My soul thirsts for You; My flesh longs for You In a dry and thirsty land Where there is no water."*
> *- Psalm 63:1 NKJV.*

Your children learn from what excites you.

Are you excited by:

- God or gold (financial gains)?

- Sermon or Sport?

- Prayer or playing?

- Church or chores?

- Family or friends?

4. **Teach your family through what you say—Proverbs 18:21; 1 Peter 3:10.**

> *Your words can make or break people, even your children, beware!*
> *- James 3:6*

- Do you affirm them or attack them with your words?

- Do you build them up or tear them down?

- Do you encourage them or discourage them?

Family should be where you are built up, not torn down.

5. **Teach your family through the heroes you respect.**

14,000 people perished after following Korah in his rebellion against Moses. Who do you honor? Have they seen you pass disrespectful comments about your Pastor or Parents?

- Everything you do sends a message to the world, especially your children.

6. Teach your family with your triumphs and your trials.

Legacy-minded fathers understand the significance of storytelling. Sharing personal experiences and lessons learned serves to connect generations. These stories provide wisdom and a healthy appreciation for your struggles and bravery to create a shared identity that children can cherish and pass on. It is not just a memory but a living narrative that continues influencing future generations.

> *"I will open my mouth in a parable; I will utter dark sayings of old, [3] Which we have heard and known, and our fathers have told us. [4] We will not hide them from their children, telling to the generation to come the praises of the LORD, And His strength, and His wonderful works that He has done"*
> *- Psalm 78:2-4 NKJV*

Since it takes the combination of the bright hours of the day and the dark hours of the night to make a full day, we must be careful to teach with both our crowns and scars.

- **Don't just teach with your success; teach with your failures, too.**

Tell them where and how you fell and how you rose again.

- What could have happened if Abraham had taught Isaac never to be intimidated by a mortal man and fall cheaply for the spirit of lying?

Maybe Isaac would not have lied before Abimelech, too, propagating the evil spirit of deception in the subsequent generation.

- What if Joseph had taught his sons that becoming distinguished in life requires a covenant faith walk with God?

Maybe the children of Ephraim would not have practiced convenient faith in their dealings with God.

> *"The children of Ephraim, being armed and carrying bows, turned back on the day of battle. [10] They did not keep the covenant of God; They refused to walk in His law."*
> *- Psalm 78:9-10 NKJV.*

- What if David had shared his regrets about a polygamous home with Solomon? The scars of incest and fratricide, witnessing needless bloodshed in his house, maybe Solomon could have avoided promiscuity and polygamy at all costs.

- What if Solomon had taught his sons that the God of Israel is the only wise God, and He gives to whoever will be humble enough to ask for it? Maybe Rehoboam (Solomon's son who succeeded him on the throne) would not have sought counsel from the wrong people, and the nation of Israel would have avoided secession and civil war.

- What if Prophet Samuel had equipped his sons with the knowledge of tarrying before the Ark of the Covenant until they heard God's voice?

Maybe greater Prophets than Samuel would have arisen from his lineage, and the people of Israel would not have demanded a king.

Teach with your actions and, when necessary, use words.

As fathers, we are the gardeners of our family's future; we must be careful to sow today the seeds that our tomorrow will thank us for.

> *"Train up a child in the way he should go, and when he is old, he will not depart from it."*
> *- Proverbs 22:6 NKJV*

Fathers, I am passionately pleading with us; let us arise and teach the next generation so that they will not repeat the blunders of the past; instead, they will take advantage of the opportunities packaged in the future and bring glory to God.

Teaching and instructing our children should include mentoring, i.e., Role Modeling.

> *Fathers must act as mentors because mentoring brings increase and advancement*
> *- Job 8:6-10.*

Young men have time and energy, but they lack wisdom. Older men have built up wisdom over the years but don't have time and energy in their favor, so the world will be much better if the older and younger generations work together.

- **Mentoring is a strategy for connecting wisdom with time to maximize the younger generation's productivity. Hence, every succeeding generation would be an improvement on the preceding one.**

When Pharaoh was negotiating with Moses, the first request was for the men to go and leave their children behind. This would have robbed an entire generation of an opportunity for mentorship, and they would have fizzled out with time. The family must grow together for continuity.

Satan, like Pharaoh, does everything to have a generation where the fathers are absent in their roles of mentorship to ensure there is no future strong enough to propagate God's agenda.

Fathers must not completely outsource the role of mentorship or teaching the next generation to the school; the school system cannot model God to them. Please take up the role of mentoring your children diligently.

Do not hide your scars; use your scars as a tool for mentoring.

Be vulnerable; do not pretend to be Superman. Your wounds could be a great asset for your children, so don't hide them.

Note that character is most demanded from you when teaching your children; don't just teach them; lead them. Love must be the core of a role-model father.

Character is important; no matter how talented or motivated someone is, it counts for nothing if they are weak in character. As the Greek philosopher Heraclitus said, character is fate. You want to ensure you are doing everything you can to help your children build character and give them a strong inner compass.

In addition, emotional availability is a hallmark of a legacy-minded father. Children develop confidence and strong character when parents are actively present and engaged in their lives, thus building secure attachment. When fathers actively listen, provide support, and show affection, they create a nurturing environment that empowers children to thrive. This emotional connection strengthens the father-child bond and teaches children the importance of healthy relationships, which they will carry into their own lives.

Building a strong family legacy

Fathers must be nurturers and encouragers. As a father, you nurture, encourage, and challenge your children to maximize their potential.

Sometimes, fathers project their unfulfilled dreams and aspirations on their children rather than allowing them to live their own dreams and aspirations; this could be discouraging and counterproductive.

> *"Those who influenced me the most are not those who pointed out all my faults, but those who knew God was bigger than my shortcomings. Those who influenced me the most didn't just point a finger; they held out a helping hand,"*

> *- Phil Callaway, Making Life Rich Without Any Money.*

The best gift you can give to your children is not a diamond but to guide them into their Diamond Mine.

Your children's divine assignment or purpose is their Diamond Mine; once you can guide them to locate their purpose and encourage and challenge them to fulfill it, greatness is inevitable. When your children are situated in their purpose, all their gifts begin to find expression. They will feel like kings from day one because that is one place where everyone acknowledges them as kings and accords them the honor they deserve.

It's in their purpose that they don't feel threatened or intimidated because they are wired to win there.

In celebrating your child, appeal to their untapped potential, not their greed or pride.

Start saying things like:

- "I have always known that there is greatness in you; if you can prepare or train for it, you can bring it forth."

- "You have all that is needed to be great."

Stop saying things like:

- "You are the best among them."

- "You must always come first."

- "What's your position?"

- "You must always top your class!"

Don't stimulate their jealousy or competitiveness. Instead, encourage their creativity and call forth their greatness by pointing them to their untapped potential.

As a father, your job is to nurture. This does not mean creating superstars, athletes, or the next in line for the family business, though that could be possible. You are to nurture your children into becoming who they are created to be. This identity ultimately comes from them. While you offer diverse activities and experiences to them, their natural inclinations will dictate their choices.

As a father, you must identify and nurture their interests and abilities as they emerge. If your son is the first in the family to be utterly uninterested in fixing cars, you may need to let him try out other things that could be of interest. You are there to help your children see whatever the world offers. They will do the rest. By forcing your child to go down a certain path, you may actually be holding them back from realizing their potential.

Never make your children feel bad or silly for liking something or expressing interest. Let them be who they are and be happy with that. That is how you nurture your child.

More so, praising your children at the slightest glimpse of their excellent work is part of encouragement because whatever you appreciate will never depreciate.

- **Look for opportunities to praise more than you rebuke; every praise fuels their flame.**

Examples of Praise Statements

- I appreciate the effort you have put in; you worked hard. Great job!

- You've come up with a lovely solution; I'm proud of you.

- I am glad you had a fantastic focus while working on this project.

- I appreciate that you left some for your brother; that was thoughtful of you.

- I appreciate that you didn't give up.

- Thank you for saying that. It means so much to me.

- I am glad you shared this with your siblings. Thanks for being selfless.

- Thank you for helping out there.

Fathers must be a Source for Continuity—As great fathers, you must be legacy-minded.

You are only as great as the great person who succeeds you.

Someone must be an extension of your effort and exploit; if not, you have failed - **Proverbs 13:22.**

The enemy invariably attacks succession: no wonder the devil used Cain to kill Abel.

"What will you give me since I go childless?"—Succession was paramount to Abraham.

These are five things that every great father must give to their descendants:

1. The First and the greatest inheritance you must give to your children is God, not gold. Any generation that you give gold without God will eventually turn the gold to god; beware!

2. Give your conviction–summation of your beliefs and philosophies (your philosophy about success, wealth, failure, relationship) - **Genesis 18:19-20.**

3. Give a good name–Your name summarizes your credibility, track record, and impact.

Name is significant to God; it is no wonder He changed people's names.

The Bible says, God, how excellent is thy name–**Psalm 8:1.**

When Jesus is mentioned, hell quakes because of the power in His name.

At the end of your life, your name can become a key that opens the door or a padlock that locks it up. It is not enough to be great; your name must be great, too, as God did for Abraham - **Genesis 12:1.**

- **When you are blessed, you enjoy the benefit alone, but when your name is great, others coming behind you can leverage the name for their greatness.**

Jesus left us His name, and we are still winning with it today. It is better to protect your name than to protect money.

4. Give your relationship and connection–**John 19:26-27.**

All blessings come from God through men to men; all troubles come from Satan through men to men. Men are prophetic midwives. God needed Mary to give birth to the Savior.

- **Invest strategically in godly and goodly relationships.**

5. Give physical assets–Land, stock, businesses, and investments. The prodigal son only received these, and he lost it all. He did not have the first four earlier mentioned.

The prodigal son did not respect his father's God, convictions, names, and relationship–**Luke 15:12.**

Being legacy-minded is the only guaranteed way to make your labor and achievements immune to waste.

> *"This is the case of a man who is all alone, without a child or a brother, yet works hard to gain as much wealth as possible. But then he asks himself, 'Who am I working for? Why am I giving up so much pleasure now?' It is all so meaningless and depressing."*
> *- Ecclesiastes 4:8 NLT*

In the scriptural passage quoted above, a picture of a man who was not legacy-minded was painted for us. This person is said to be alone and has neither a son nor a brother. The first point I observed is that this man did not drop from the sky. He had a father, which indicates that someone in the past generation had taken the time to mentor him. (The past generation represents the father who has taken time to pour virtues and knowledge into him).

This man quoted in this scriptural passage began to observe that his labor would most likely end up as a waste because he had failed to mentor anyone (not pouring knowledge and virtues into others). He was not mentoring (pouring into or impacting) anyone in the present (brothers or contemporaries), nor was he mentoring the future, which represents a child (pouring into or impacting anyone that will propagate his legacy in the future). This child must not be biological alone; he could be an adopted child or a protégé.

Everything he owned and knew would most likely die with him; what a wasted life!

It is essential to have a mindset of a river; we collect from many others and pass it on for a more significant impact. The mentality of a lake can be deadly; the lake receives everything but never releases it, and the end product is deadness, stench, and stagnancy.

Intentional fathering, as detailed in this chapter, prioritizes relationship-building with children over simply enforcing rules.

Fathers must be legacy-minded to ensure that their influence endures beyond their years. Fathers can create a profound and lasting impact on their children by instilling values, fostering traditions, prioritizing education, being emotionally available, and sharing stories. The legacy they leave will shape not only their children's lives but also the lives of those who come after them, making the role of a father one of the most significant contributions to society. In cultivating a legacy, fathers honor their own journey and empower their children to embark on their own, enriched by the lessons and love passed down through generations.

> *"Being a great father is like shaving. No matter how good you shaved today, you must do it again tomorrow."*
> *- Reed Markham*

You do not finish the work of parenting as the mentoring part of it continues until you leave this world.

I'm not insinuating that these responsibilities are easy to do, but with the help of the Father of all fathers, it can be done, and it must be done. Why?

This is because your children are the letters you are writing into the future, and what you write in them today is what the world will read in them tomorrow. So, what are you writing in them?

Will the future generation praise you after meeting and reading your children, or will they curse you for the monster and disaster you have packaged and sent to them? Think about that.

TIME FOR REflECTION

1. What do you find most captivating in this chapter?

____

____

____

____

____

2. Based on the new insights gained, what commitment(s) will you make?

____

____

____

____

____

3. What are your action steps to implement your commitment(s)?

____

____

____

____

____

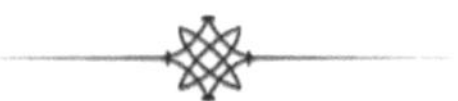

A Desperate Call to Rise

> *"Any fool can have a child. That doesn't make you a father. It's the courage to raise a child that makes you a father."*
> **- Barack Obama.**

This book is never intended to make light the demands of fatherhood; it is simply a desperate call from a very concerned father who believes that if our consciousness is awakened to the dangers and demands of a fatherless society, it could stir up the passion to arise and become intentional about our fatherhood roles.

In contemporary society, the roles of fathers have evolved, yet the call for responsible fatherhood remains as urgent as ever. The absence of responsible fathers can have profound implications for families and communities, leading to a cycle of emotional and social challenges.

A desperate call for responsible fathers highlights the need for engaged, nurturing, and accountable male figures in the lives of children, as their presence significantly influences the next generation's emotional, psychological, and social development. One of the most pressing reasons for this call is the alarming statistics surrounding the father's absence.

Research indicates that children who grow up without a father figure are more likely to face a range of adversities, including higher rates of poverty, academic struggles, and behavioral issues. These children often lack the emotional support and guidance that a responsible father provides. The absence of a father can lead to feelings of abandonment and low self-worth, affecting a child's ability to form healthy relationships later in life.

Thus, responsible fathers who actively participate in their children's lives are needed to foster emotional resilience and stability.

In addition to emotional support, responsible fathers play a crucial role in the education and development of their children. Fathers who are engaged in their children's learning enhance academic achievement and instill a love for knowledge and curiosity. They serve as role models, demonstrating the value of hard work, perseverance, and integrity.

The desperate call for responsible fathers emphasizes the importance of active involvement in their children's education, whether through attending school events, helping with homework, or encouraging a growth mindset. This involvement benefits the children and strengthens the father-child relationship, creating lasting bonds built on trust and respect.

Furthermore, responsible fatherhood contributes to the overall well-being of families and communities. Fathers who take their responsibilities seriously help create a stable and nurturing home environment.

This stability is fundamental for healthy family dynamics and reduces the likelihood of family conflicts and dysfunction. Communities with engaged fathers often see lower crime rates and improved social cohesion. The call for responsible fathers is, therefore, a plea for individual families and a call to action for communities to foster supportive networks that encourage and empower fathers to take an active role in their children's lives.

Moreover, the redefining of masculinity in modern society plays a significant role in this desperate call. Traditional notions of masculinity often emphasize stoicism and emotional detachment, which can hinder a father's ability to connect with his children. However, the contemporary understanding of masculinity encourages emotional openness and vulnerability. Responsible fathers embrace these qualities, allowing them to engage more meaningfully with their children. This shift is crucial for breaking down the barriers that prevent fathers from being present and emotionally available.

Fatherhood is never something that perfect men do, but something that perfects the man who embarks on the journey.

Every father may be unable to do great things by the standard of the Guinness Book of Records and Nobel Prize Awarding Institutions. Still, every father can raise great sons, sons who will remain unforgettable in men's hearts, even if no street is named after them.

The greatest disaster is not for one to live and die but for one to be dead while living. One of the signs that a tree is dead is fruitlessness—when nothing is coming out of the tree to ensure its continuity, as the seed of the future is in the fruit of the present.

The same goes for fathers with no seed of investment in their sons to perpetuate their names, values, and all they have labored for. They are likened to an ostrich, as stated below:

> *"She treats her young harshly, as though they were not hers. Her labor is in vain, without concern, [17] Because God deprived her of wisdom and did not endow her with understanding,"*
> *- Job 39:16-17 NKJV.*

We cannot afford to be Ostrich-like fathers, paying little or no attention to our children. These children are our future, and if we ignore the opportunity to arise and train them, we could just be toiling with a mega regret in the future.

Whatever labor (business, ministry, or career) preoccupies us now, which is not allowing us to give our children the much-needed attention, that labor could amount to vanity if little or no investment is made in our children.

In his book The Daily Dad, Ryan Holiday says, "Just a few generations ago, having a child was seen as an investment in your future. Keep them alive through the difficult bit, and you'll eventually have an able set of hands to help you work the land. The idea of providing emotional care or unconditional love was a luxury that the times didn't always allow."

Unfortunately, many parents, particularly fathers, are denied an active emotional presence in their children's lives today because of their hustle.

Do you think you are too busy? Take note:

"Raising sons is much easier than repairing broken men."

An African proverb says, *"It's better to trim the branch of an Iroko tree going off course while it's young. If it becomes mature, it will become a god, and you will need to appease it with regular sacrifice before it can be trimmed."*

This proverb is a warning that we need to correct our children when they are young before the situation gets out of hand. It says it's much better to address a challenging situation in our children while fresh, as it may become a painful problem that would bring heartache later.

Untamed children become increasingly difficult to manage as they mature; proactive training is essential.

There is an African proverb that says, "A child you don't build will squander away cheaply whatever empire you have built."

Fathers, we need to be wise; it is foolish to be busy building something today that will be wasted tomorrow by the children we fail to build today.

We must engage the power of the Holy Spirit and foresight to balance our investment in our "Interprise" (Business of building family) and Enterprise (Business, Career, or Ministry).

> *"And Jeremiah said to the house of the Rechabites, "Thus says the LORD of hosts, the God of Israel: 'Because you have obeyed the commandment of Jonadab, your father, and kept all his precepts and done according to all that he commanded you, [19] therefore thus says the LORD of hosts, the God of Israel: "Jonadab the son of Rechab shall not lack a man to stand before Me forever"*
> *- Jeremiah 35:18-19 NKJV.*

The Bible passage quoted above is the story of the Rechabites dynasty.

They were known for their strict adherence to the instructions handed down by their ancestors, which included not drinking wine, not participating in agriculture, and not engaging in other Canaanite practices. The Rechabites were devout followers of the God of Israel and are also known for their involvement in the revolt led by Jehu to kill the worshippers of Baal (Idol).

God praised the Rechabites for their loyalty to their family values and promised that the descendants of the Rechabites would always enjoy the blessing given to their lineage.

Fathers, what instructions (values) are we giving our children to enhance the continuity of God's blessings (His Presence, Peace, Provisions, and Protection) in our families?

If there is none yet, don't beat yourself down. This book has found its way into your hands so you can hear this desperate call to arise as a father and begin to do the needful.

This is a clarion call for societal change. It underscores the critical need for engaged, nurturing, and accountable fathers who can profoundly impact their children's lives. By fostering emotional resilience, enhancing educational outcomes, and promoting stable family environments, responsible fathers contribute to healthier communities and a brighter future for future generations.

It is imperative that society collectively supports and empower fathers in their roles, recognizing that responsible fatherhood is not just a personal responsibility but a vital societal necessity.

Fathers, let's arise to instruct the next generation in godly values that will keep them stable and steady; these instructions will guarantee the perpetuation of God's blessings on our dynasties.

There is obviously no time any longer. Why should we wait any further? It's time, Fathers, Arise!

FATHER'S PRAYER:

Thank God for the privilege of fatherhood and the opportunity to link the last and the next generation together. Thank God for the chance to inherit the past, refine it in the present, and leave a legacy for the next generation to propagate.

Passionately pray the following:

- Lord, help me to be a father strong enough to know my weaknesses and brave enough to face my fears as I engage my strengths.

- Lord, help me to be a proud and unbending father in a challenging situation but humble and gentle in victory.

- Lord, help me to be a father who is righteous yet relatable, firm yet friendly, compelling in my convictions yet compassionate, thorough yet thoughtful, powerful yet patient, and great yet gracious to all.

- Lord, help me to be a father who is vulnerable enough to know that I can do nothing on my own but daring enough to challenge my giants, knowing that I can do all things through Christ who strengthens me.

- Lord, give me the courage to withstand the storms necessary to build my faith so I can have compassion for those being challenged by the storm later, too.

- Lord, help me to be a father whose heart is clean and whose goals are high.

- Lord, help me to be a father who will master himself before he seeks to master other people; a father who will learn to laugh yet not forget how to weep; a father who will reach into the future without forgetting the lessons of the past.

- Lord, help me to be a father with a good sense of humor so that despite my seriousness, I will never take myself too seriously.

- Give me humility so I may never forget the simplicity of greatness, the open-mindedness of true wisdom, and the humility of true strength.

- Lord, give me wisdom not to clone my children but to empower them to be authentic as they unlock their potential.

- Endow me with the grace to raise a family where God is feared, loved, and served.

- Lord, help me live so well that I will be an example for the next generation, not a mistake to avoid.

- Lord, help me model God, the Father, genuinely not to misrepresent Him so that the generations coming behind me will never have a reason to desire another god.

- Grant me answers to all these prayers so that when I look back at my life, I can confidently declare I have not lived in vain.

In Jesus' mighty name, I pray - Amen!

TIME FOR REflECTION

1. What do you find most captivating in this chapter?

____

____

____

____

____

2. Based on the new insights gained, what commitment(s) will you make?

____

____

____

____

____

3. What are your action steps to implement your commitment(s)?

____

____

____

____

____

Conclusion

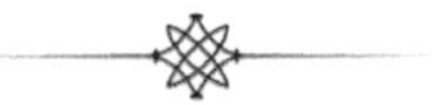

> *"A father is neither an anchor to hold us back nor a sail to take us there, but a guiding light whose love shows us the way."*
> **- Unknown.**

The Bible likens children to different things: seeds, God's heritage, arrows, and the like. Children being arrows will need an archer's skillfulness and present-mindedness to hit their targets in life. Fathers are archers urgently required to launch different arrows into the future to hit the target.

"Fathers, Arise" is a call to God's stewards (fathers) to avert fatherlessness - the pandemic that threatens human existence more than all the world-power nuclear weapons put together.

Fatherhood is never something that perfect men do, but something that perfects the man who embarks on the journey.

There is a likelihood that every father may be unable to do great things according to the standards of the Guinness Book of Records and Nobel Prize Awarding Institutions. Still, every father can raise their children in a significant way that will make them unforgettable in the hearts of men.

"Fathers Arise!" is a rallying cry that resonates deeply in contemporary society, emphasizing the critical role fathers need to play in the lives of their children and communities. This phrase encapsulates a call to action for fathers to step into their roles with dedication, purpose, and awareness of the profound impact they can have on their children and society at large.

The importance of fatherhood extends beyond mere presence; it encompasses emotional support, guidance, and cultivating a nurturing environment.

This book explores the pressing need for fathers to arise and be more present in their children's lives, highlighting the benefits of paternal involvement and the consequences of a father's absence. One of the most significant reasons for the urgent need for fathers to engage actively in their children's lives is the impact of fatherhood on a child's emotional and psychological development. Research indicates that children with involved fathers exhibit higher self-esteem, better social skills, and improved academic performance.

Fathers provide unique perspectives and skills that complement maternal care, contributing to a more balanced upbringing. The absence of a father can lead to feelings of abandonment and insecurity, which can manifest in behavioral issues and difficulties in forming healthy relationships.

Lastly, the call for fathers to arise is a powerful reminder of their vital role in shaping the future. Fathers can significantly impact their children's lives and the broader community by embracing their responsibilities with passion and commitment. The fatherhood journey is filled with challenges but rich with opportunities for growth, connection, and transformation. As society continues to evolve, we must recognize and support the importance of fathers, encouraging them to take their rightful place as active, and nurturing figures in their children's lives.

About The Author

Kola is a dynamic, passionate, and anointed teacher of the Word with a deep hunger to see the truth of God's Word simplified and accessible to all.

He is a love practitioner, speaker, and writer, and an incurable optimist convinced that everyone's potential must be developed to unleash their talents, bettering the world and bringing glory to God.

Kola was trained as a business administrator and served in the industry for several years before accepting the divine call as a full-time minister of the gospel.

His unique background allows him to bridge the gap between spirituality and humanity with ease. The practical life applications from his teachings equip his audience to win with the word in every area of endeavor.

He is blessed to be under the tutelage of visionary leaders and Pastors–Pastor Toye & Wumi Ademola, the Presiding Pastors of Dominion International Center, with headquarters in Houston, Texas, and several other branches across the globe.

Kola currently serves as the Lead Pastor of Dominion International Center, Cypress, a young, vibrant, growing church in the Northwest side of Houston, Texas.

He hosts young men for mentorship on his online platform–"Real Men Talk" and leads the church to host an annual conference tagged, "Fathers, Arise!"; a meeting where men are equipped with the truth of God's word to rise up to the challenges of fatherhood in the 21st century.

Outside of his pastoral duties, Kola is a family man to the core, who loves investing quality time in his "four young generals and wife," engages in community service, believing that faith should be actionable. He enjoys mentoring young men and is passionate about fostering an inclusive environment where everybody feels like somebody because we are all nobodies saved by His grace.

Kola is excited about the future and always looks forward to leading his audience on a journey of faith, growth, and service to be pacesetters and role models.